791.43　　　　　　　　　　　109110
Shu

　　Shuttleworth.
　　The social conduct and attitudes of
　　　movie fans.

The Library
Nazareth College of Rochester, N. Y.

The Literature of Cinema

ADVISORY EDITOR: **MARTIN S. DWORKIN**
INSTITUTE OF PHILOSOPHY AND POLITICS OF EDUCATION
TEACHER'S COLLEGE, COLUMBIA UNIVERSITY

THE LITERATURE OF CINEMA presents a comprehensive selection from the multitude of writings about cinema, rediscovering materials on its origins, history, theoretical principles and techniques, aesthetics, economics, and effects on societies and individuals. Included are works of inherent, lasting merit and others of primarily historical significance. These provide essential resources for serious study and critical enjoyment of the "magic shadows" that became one of the decisive cultural forces of modern times.

The Social Conduct and Attitudes of Movie Fans

Frank K. Shuttleworth and Mark A. May

Motion Pictures and the Social Attitudes of Children

Ruth C. Peterson and L. L. Thurstone

ARNO PRESS & THE NEW YORK TIMES
New York • 1970

Reprint Edition 1970 by Arno Press Inc.
Library of Congress Catalog Card Number: 79-125463
ISBN 0-405-01630-1
ISBN for complete set: 0-405-01600-X
Manufactured in the United States of America

MOTION PICTURES
AND THE SOCIAL ATTITUDES
OF CHILDREN

———

THE SOCIAL CONDUCT AND
ATTITUDES OF MOVIE FANS

MOTION PICTURES AND YOUTH

THE PAYNE FUND STUDIES

W. W. CHARTERS, CHAIRMAN

MOTION PICTURES AND YOUTH: A SUMMARY, by W. W. Charters, Director, Bureau of Educational Research, Ohio State University.

Combined with

GETTING IDEAS FROM THE MOVIES, by P. W. Holaday, Indianapolis Public Schools, and George D. Stoddard, Director, Iowa Child Welfare Research Station.

MOTION PICTURES AND THE SOCIAL ATTITUDES OF CHILDREN, by Ruth C. Peterson and L. L. Thurstone, Department of Psychology, University of Chicago.

Combined with

THE SOCIAL CONDUCT AND ATTITUDES OF MOVIE FANS, by Frank K. Shuttleworth and Mark A. May, Institute of Human Relations, Yale University.

THE EMOTIONAL RESPONSES OF CHILDREN TO THE MOTION PICTURE SITUATION, by W. S. Dysinger and Christian A. Ruckmick, Department of Psychology, State University of Iowa.

Combined with

MOTION PICTURES AND STANDARDS OF MORALITY, by Charles C. Peters, Professor of Education, Pennsylvania State College.

CHILDREN'S SLEEP, by Samuel Renshaw, Vernon L. Miller, and Dorothy Marquis, Department of Psychology, Ohio State University.

MOVIES AND CONDUCT, by Herbert Blumer, Department of Sociology, University of Chicago.

THE CONTENT OF MOTION PICTURES, by Edgar Dale, Research Associate, Bureau of Educational Research, Ohio State University.

Combined with

CHILDREN'S ATTENDANCE AT MOTION PICTURES, by Edgar Dale.

MOVIES, DELINQUENCY, AND CRIME, by Herbert Blumer and Philip M. Hauser, Department of Sociology, University of Chicago.

BOYS, MOVIES, AND CITY STREETS, by Paul G. Cressey and Frederick M. Thrasher, New York University.

HOW TO APPRECIATE MOTION PICTURES, by Edgar Dale, Research Associate, Bureau of Educational Research, Ohio State University.

MOTION PICTURES AND THE SOCIAL ATTITUDES OF CHILDREN

❖

RUTH C. PETERSON
UNIVERSITY OF CHICAGO

L. L. THURSTONE
PROFESSOR OF PSYCHOLOGY
UNIVERSITY OF CHICAGO

NEW YORK
THE MACMILLAN COMPANY
1933

THIS SERIES OF TWELVE STUDIES OF THE INFLUENCE OF MOTION PICTURES UPON CHILDREN AND YOUTH HAS BEEN MADE BY THE COMMITTEE ON EDUCATIONAL RESEARCH OF THE PAYNE FUND AT THE REQUEST OF THE NATIONAL COMMITTEE FOR THE STUDY OF SOCIAL VALUES IN MOTION PICTURES, NOW THE MOTION PICTURE RESEARCH COUNCIL, 366 MADISON AVENUE, NEW YORK CITY. THE STUDIES WERE DESIGNED TO SECURE AUTHORITATIVE AND IMPERSONAL DATA WHICH WOULD MAKE POSSIBLE A MORE COMPLETE EVALUATION OF MOTION PICTURES AND THEIR SOCIAL POTENTIALITIES

COPYRIGHT, 1933,

BY THE MACMILLAN COMPANY

All rights reserved—no part of this book may be reproduced in any form without permission in writing from the publisher, except by a reviewer who wishes to quote brief passages in connection with a review written for inclusion in magazine or newspaper.

Set up and printed from type. Published November, 1933.

PRINTED IN THE UNITED STATES OF AMERICA

CHAIRMAN'S PREFACE

MOTION PICTURES are not understood by the present generation of adults. They are new; they make an enormous appeal to children; and they present ideas and situations which parents may not like. Consequently when parents think of the welfare of their children who are exposed to these compelling situations, they wonder about the effect of the pictures upon the ideals and behavior of the children. Do the pictures really influence children in any direction? Are their conduct, ideals, and attitudes affected by the movies? Are the scenes which are objectionable to adults understood by children, or at least by very young children? Do children eventually become sophisticated and grow superior to pictures? Are the emotions of children harmfully excited? In short, just what effect do motion pictures have upon children of different ages?

Each individual has his answer to these questions. He knows of this or that incident in his own experience, and upon these he bases his conclusions. Consequently opinions differ widely. No one in this country up to the present time has known in any general and impersonal manner just what effect motion pictures have upon children. Meanwhile children clamor to attend the movies as often as they are allowed to go. Moving pictures make a profound appeal to children of all ages. In such a situation it is obvious that a comprehensive study of the influence of motion pictures upon children and youth is appropriate.

To measure these influences the investigators who coöperated to make this series of studies analyzed the problem to discover the most significant questions involved. They set up individual studies to ascertain the answer to the questions and to provide a composite answer to the central question of the nature and extent of these influences. In using this technique the answers must inevitably be sketches without all the details filled in; but when the details are added the picture will not be changed in any essential manner. Parents, educators, and physicians will have little difficulty in fitting concrete details of their own into the outlines which these studies supply.

Specifically, the studies were designed to form a series to answer the following questions: What sorts of scenes do the children of America see when they attend the theaters? How do the mores depicted in these scenes compare with those of the community? How often do children attend? How much of what they see do they remember? What effect does what they witness have upon their ideals and attitudes? Upon their sleep and health? Upon their emotions? Do motion pictures directly or indirectly affect the conduct of children? Are they related to delinquency and crime, and, finally, how can we teach children to discriminate between movies that are artistically and morally good and bad?

The history of the investigations is brief. In 1928 William H. Short, Executive Director of the Motion Picture Research Council, invited a group of university psychologists, sociologists, and educators to meet with the members of the Council to confer about the possibility of discovering just what effect motion pictures have upon children, a subject, as has been indicated, upon which many conflicting opinions and few substantial facts were in existence. The university men proposed a program of study. When Mr. Short appealed to The Payne Fund for a grant to support

CHAIRMAN'S PREFACE

such an investigation, he found the foundation receptive because of its well-known interest in motion pictures as one of the major influences in the lives of modern youth. When the appropriation had been made the investigators organized themselves into a Committee on Educational Research of The Payne Fund with the following membership: L. L. Thurstone, Frank N. Freeman, R. E. Park, Herbert Blumer, Philip M. Hauser of the University of Chicago; George D. Stoddard, Christian A. Ruckmick, P. W. Holaday, and Wendell Dysinger of the University of Iowa; Mark A. May and Frank K. Shuttleworth of Yale University; Frederick M. Thrasher and Paul G. Cressey of New York University; Charles C. Peters of Pennsylvania State College; Ben D. Wood of Columbia University; and Samuel Renshaw, Edgar Dale, and W. W. Charters of Ohio State University. The investigations have extended through four years, 1929–1932 inclusive.

The committee's work is an illustration of an interesting technique for studying any social problem. The distinctive characteristic of this technique is to analyze a complex social problem into a series of subordinate problems, to select competent investigators to work upon each of the subordinate projects and to integrate the findings of all the investigators as a solution of the initial problem. Such a program yields a skeleton framework, which, while somewhat lacking in detail, is substantially correct if the contributing investigations have been validly conducted. To provide this framework or outline is the task of research. To fill in the detail and to provide the interpretations are the natural and easy tasks of those who use the data.

W. W. C.

Columbus, Ohio
June, 1933

AUTHORS' PREFACE

THIS series of experimental studies on the effect of motion pictures on social attitudes, made possible by a grant from the Payne Fund, has been carried out under the general direction of Professor W. W. Charters of Ohio State University. We are especially indebted to him for his continued interest and support. We wish to acknowledge the assistance of Mr. W. H. Short, Director of the Motion Picture Research Council (formerly the National Committee for the Study of Social Values in Motion Pictures).

The success of these studies was dependent upon the interest and coöperation of a large number of people. We wish to thank Professor W. C. Reavis of the University of Chicago for suggesting the superintendents and principals who coöperated with us in this study. The suggestions and help of Thelma Gwinn Thurstone have been most valuable. We wish to acknowledge the assistance of Helen Liebermann, Leone Chesire, Catherine Hawkins Opler, and Dorothy Blumenstock in the tabulation and calculation of the data. All of the motion-picture distributing agencies in Chicago assisted us greatly by giving us press sheets of their films and by making special arrangements for bookings and previews. Mr. Nelson L. Greene, Editor of *The Educational Screen*, suggested a number of films for our studies. We wish to thank Mr. F. M. Clarke of Clarke-McElroy Printing Company and the University of Chicago Press for facilitating the experiments by prompt printing of the necessary forms.

We wish to express our appreciation to the following superintendents and principals for their generous interest and coöperation in this study.

Mr. H. B. Loomis, Principal of Hyde Park High School, Chicago, Illinois.

Sister De Lellis, Principal of Thomas Aquinas High School, Chicago, Illinois.

Mr. Cloy S. Hobson, Principal of Genoa Township High School, Genoa, Illinois.

Mr. M. E. Steele, Principal of Mendota Township High School, Mendota, Illinois.

Mr. O. V. Shaffer, Principal of Princeton Township High School, Princeton, Illinois.

Mr. H. M. Coultrap, Superintendent of Geneva Public Schools, Geneva, Illinois.

Mr. C. C. Byerly, Principal of West Chicago Community High School, West Chicago, Illinois.

Mr. James D. Darnall, Principal of Geneseo Township High School, Geneseo, Illinois.

Mr. H. C. Storm, Superintendent of Batavia Public Schools, Batavia, Illinois.

Mr. Albert Britt, President of Knox College, Galesburg, Illinois.

Mr. Rutledge T. Wiltbank, Professor of Psychology, Knox College, Galesburg, Illinois.

Mr. E. W. Powers, Principal of Watseka Community High School, Watseka, Illinois.

Mr. John J. Swinney, Principal of Paxton Community High School, Paxton, Illinois.

Mr. L. C. McCarty, Superintendent of Aledo Public Schools, Aledo, Illinois.

Mr. R. E. Dahl, Principal of Aledo Junior High School, Aledo, Illinois.

Mr. H. A. Dean, Superintendent of Crystal Lake Public Schools, Crystal Lake, Illinois.

The experiments conducted at Mooseheart were made possible through the interest and assistance given by Mr. Ernest N. Roselle, Superintendent, Mr. Martin L. Reymert, Director of Mooseheart Laboratory for Child Research, Mr. V. Q. Bird, Director of Education, and Mr. L. A. Meyer, Research Assistant.

Mr. Burton Holmes and the manager of the Burton Holmes Lectures assisted us in arranging for the experiment carried on with the coöperation of Thomas Aquinas High School.

The following theater owners and managers have assisted us greatly by making special arrangements for motion-picture films and by changing their bookings for our convenience.

Mr. Ezra Levin, Tower Theatre, Chicago, Illinois.

Mr. Albert Awe of Genoa Theatre, Genoa, Illinois.

Mr. A. M. Robertson of The Strand Theatre, Mendota, Illinois.

Mr. Jerome Rieth of The Apollo Theatre, Princeton, Illinois.

Mr. Paul Polka of Polka Brothers Theatres, Maywood, Illinois.

Mr. Jack Greene of Geneseo Theatre, Geneseo, Illinois.

Mr. Joe Burke of Vanity Theatre, Batavia, Illinois.

Mr. T. J. McSpadden of West Colonial Theatre, Galesburg, Illinois.

Mr. F. E. Fanning of Crystal Theatre, Watseka, Illinois.

Mr. C. O. Greenwood of Paxtonian Theatre, Paxton, Illinois.

Mr. J. W. Edwards of Aledo Opera House, Aledo, Illinois.

Mrs. Butler of El Tovar Theatre, Crystal Lake, Illinois.

Authors' Preface

The following attitude scales were used in this study by permission of the authors:

1. The scale, *Attitude toward War*, which was used in the experiment at Genoa, Illinois, was constructed by Mr. D. D. Droba.
2. The scale, *Attitude toward War*, which was used in the experiments at Batavia, Paxton, and Mooseheart, Illinois, was constructed by Ruth C. Peterson.
3. The scale, *Attitude toward the German People*, which was used in the experiment at Genoa, Illinois, was constructed by Ruth C. Peterson.
4. The scale, *Attitude toward Prohibition*, which was used in the experiment at Princeton, Illinois, was constructed by Hattie Nesbitt Smith.
5. The scale, *Attitude toward Chinese*, which was used in the experiments at Geneva and West Chicago, Illinois, was constructed by Ruth C. Peterson.
6. The scale, *Attitude toward Punishment of Criminals*, which was used in the experiments at Geneseo, Galesburg, Watseka, and Mooseheart, Illinois, was constructed by Charles K. A. Wang and L. L. Thurstone.
7. The scale, *Attitude toward Capital Punishment*, which was used in the experiment at Aledo, Illinois, was constructed by Ruth C. Peterson.
8. The scale, *Attitude toward the Negro*, which was used in the experiment at Crystal Lake, Illinois, was constructed by Mr. E. D. Hinckley.

R. C. P.
L. L. T.

Chicago, Illinois
January, 1933

CONTENTS

CHAPTER	PAGE
I. PRELIMINARY STUDIES	1
II. THE EFFECT OF SINGLE PICTURES	5
1. *Four Sons* and the Germans	5
2. *Four Sons* and war	10
3. *Street of Chance* and gambling	13
4. *Hide Out* and prohibition	15
5. *Son of the Gods, Welcome Danger,* and the Chinese	17
6. *The Valiant* and capital punishment	21
7. *Journey's End* and war	24
8. *All Quiet on the Western Front* and war	26
9. *The Criminal Code* and punishment of criminals	28
10. *Alibi* and punishment of criminals	33
11. *The Birth of a Nation* and the Negro	35
III. THE CUMULATIVE EFFECT OF PICTURES	39
1. Attitude toward war	39
2. Three crime pictures and the punishment of criminals	44
IV. THE PERSISTENCE OF EFFECT	51
1. Attitude toward Germans	51
2. Attitude toward Chinese	53
3. Attitude toward gambling	55
4. Attitude toward punishment of criminals	57
5. Attitude toward war	58
6. Attitude toward the Negro	60
7. Mooseheart experiments	61
V. CONCLUSIONS	64
Appendix	67
Index	75

INTRODUCTION

The experiments herewith reported were carried on to study the effect of motion pictures on the social attitudes of high school children. The effect of a motion picture on attitude toward nationality, race, crime, war, capital punishment, prohibition, and the punishment of criminals has been studied.

Briefly, the procedure has been to measure the attitude of a group of students by means of an attitude scale or a paired comparison schedule, to show the group a motion picture which has been judged as having affective value on the issue in question, and to measure the attitude of the group again the day after the picture has been shown.

It is quite obvious that a suitable motion picture is the first essential of such an experiment. A suitable picture is one which pertains definitely to some issue such as those enumerated above; secondly, it is one which we can ask high school superintendents to send their students to see; and thirdly, the picture must be fairly recent and well made so that children will not be distracted by the fashions and photography of the picture. Suggestions of possible films were obtained from a number of sources. The pictures we used were chosen by reviewing between six and eight hundred films. By saying that we reviewed that number we do not mean to imply that we saw all of them, but press sheets, which include the advertising copy and synopses of the film, were obtained from the motion-picture distributors and were carefully scrutinized. These synopses are not for publication but are intended to give the exhibitors a fairly good idea of the picture. Consequently they were quite serviceable to us. The pictures which appeared from the synopses to have possibilities for use in the experiments, were seen by a committee of three or four. By this process, films were chosen which seemed to satisfy the criteria given.

The second essential is an instrument for measuring attitude. The paired comparison schedule or attitude scale used in each experiment is given in the report of that experiment. The paired comparison schedules used to measure attitude toward nationality and crime, and four of the attitude scales used, were constructed especially for these experiments. The scales, which were already available and which were suitable for use with the motion pictures chosen, were used by permission of the authors.

The construction of an attitude scale is described in connection with the scale of attitude toward motion pictures, which is given in the last section of this report.

The experimental groups vary in age and grade range, including children of the fourth to the eight grades, high school students, and in one experiment, college students. These groups were available through the coöperation of the principals and superintendents of the schools.

The general plan of the experiments was as follows. A scale of attitude was given in the school. After the scale was given the students were told that the scale would be given again after an interval of about two weeks. No direct connection was made between the application of the attitude scale and the presentation of the film. The interval between the first application of the scale and the motion picture varied slightly, but was in general about two weeks. Tickets which were printed especially were distributed in the school the day the film was shown; and these tickets were signed by the students and presented for admittance to the theater. By this means, it was possible to have an accurate record of which students attended the picture. Only the students who attended the showing of the film and who filled in the attitude scale both before and after were included in the experimental group. The scale of attitude was given in the school the morning following the presentation of the motion picture.

The experiments reported in this paper include studies of the effect of a single motion picture on attitudes, the cumulative effect of two or more pictures pertaining to the same issue, the difference in the effect of a motion picture on groups of different ages, and the persistence of the effect of the motion pictures.

MOTION PICTURES AND THE SOCIAL ATTITUDES OF CHILDREN

CHAPTER I

PRELIMINARY STUDIES

THE first experiment was conducted in April, 1929, with the coöperation of Hyde Park High School and the Tower Theater of Chicago. The experiment was set up to study the effect of motion pictures on the children's attitudes toward race and nationality. The attitudes of the high school students toward a number of nationalities were measured by a paired comparison schedule given on April 22, 1929. The directions and a sample of the schedule appear below.

AN EXPERIMENTAL STUDY OF RACIAL ATTITUDES

Write your name here_____
Boy or girl_____
Father born in_____ Mother born in_____
     (Name of country)   (Name of country)

This is an experimental study of attitudes toward races and nationalities. You are asked merely to underline the one nationality, or race, of each pair that you would rather associate with. For example, the first pair is:

Englishman—South American

If, in general, you prefer to associate with Englishmen rather than with South Americans, underline *Englishman*. If you prefer, in general, to associate with South Americans, underline

South American. If you find it difficult to decide for any pair, simply underline one of them anyway. If two nationalities are about equally well liked, they will have about the same number of underlinings in all of the papers. Be sure to underline one of each pair even if you have to make a sort of guess.

Englishman—South American
Japanese—Jew
Swede—Belgian
Russian—Armenian
Belgian—Negro
Japanese—Spaniard
Spaniard—Chinaman
Jew—Hindu

Negro—Pole
Hollander—Scotchman
Irishman—Russian
Austrian— Pole
Greek—Jew
Frenchman—Russian
Austrian—Japanese
Jew—Italian

There were 23 nationalities in the list and a total of 237 comparisons of the type indicated above.

During the following week, which was the week of spring vacation, four motion pictures were shown at special performances at the Tower Theater. The children had been given tickets which were to be signed and presented for admittance to the theater. The films shown were:

(1) "The Jazz-Singer," chosen as a picture which might affect the children's attitudes toward the Jews, shown on April 29.
(2) "Michael Strogoff," chosen as a picture which might affect the children's attitudes toward the Russians, shown on April 30.
(3 & 4) "Four Sons" and "The Emden," two pictures which might affect attitude toward the Germans, shown on May 1 and May 2 respectively.

The paired comparison schedule was given again at the school the following Monday, May 6. As indicated in the directions, the children were asked to underline the nationality of each pair which they preferred to associate with. The results were tabulated, and the proportion of students who preferred nationality A to nationality B was calculated for each pair. With these proportions, the scale value of each nationality was calculated by the law of comparative judgment. These scale values, representing the attitudes of the children toward each nationality before they saw the motion pictures, were compared with scale values similarly calculated for the group after they saw the motion pictures. The shifts in attitude were in general in the expected direction, but the differences were not statistically significant.

Considering the fact that it was difficult to obtain pictures which had not previously played in theaters which were available to the students in a Chicago high school, it was thought advisable to carry on the subsequent experiments in small towns where the children are less sophisticated as far as motion pictures are concerned and where the population is more homogeneous. With the exception of the study at Thomas Aquinas High School, the rest of the experiments were carried on in small towns in Illinois.

In the second experiment, a group of children from Thomas Aquinas High School were invited to the Burton Holmes lecture on Italy which was given in Orchestra Hall, Chicago, on March 15, 1930. A paired comparison of nationalities, of which the following is a sample, was given in the school the week previous to the lecture and was given in Orchestra Hall immediately after the lecture. In this case each of the 14 nationalities was paired with every other, making a total of 91 comparisons.

A STUDY OF NATIONALITY PREFERENCES

Write your name here⎯⎯⎯⎯⎯⎯⎯⎯⎯⎯⎯⎯⎯⎯⎯⎯⎯⎯⎯⎯
Boy or girl⎯⎯⎯⎯⎯⎯⎯⎯⎯⎯⎯⎯⎯
Father born in⎯⎯⎯⎯⎯⎯⎯⎯⎯ Mother born in⎯⎯⎯⎯⎯⎯⎯⎯⎯
         (Name of country)   (Name of country)

This is a study of attitudes toward nationalities. You are asked to underline the one nationality of each pair that you would rather associate with. For example, the first pair is:

Englishman—Armenian

If, in general, you prefer to associate with Englishmen rather than with Armenians, underline *Englishman*. If you prefer, in general, to associate with Armenians, underline *Armenian*. If you find it difficult to decide for any pair, be sure to underline one of them anyway. If two nationalities are about equally well liked, they will have about the same number of underlinings in all of the papers. Be sure to underline one of each pair even if you have to guess.

Englishman—Armenian	Greek—Pole
Swede—Belgian	German—Austrian
Russian—Armenian	Irishman—German
Armenian—Italian	Irishman—Belgian
Armenian—Irish	Swede—Armenian
Swede—Russian	Greek—Irishman
Russian—Austrian	Irishman—Frenchman
Armenian—Spaniard	German—Armenian

The experiment showed a slight change in attitude favorable to Italians, but the change was not statistically significant. The experiment was incidental, but was carried on because the subjects and lecture were readily available.

CHAPTER II

THE EFFECT OF SINGLE PICTURES

"Four Sons" and the Germans

The first of a series of experiments carried on in small towns was conducted in Genoa, Illinois, a town with a population of about 1,200.[1] The experimental group consisted of 133 children in grades seven to twelve inclusive. With the coöperation of Mr. Cloy S. Hobson, principal of the Genoa Township High School, the following three schedules were given in the school on April 17, 1930:

(1) a scale of attitude toward Germans.
(2) a paired comparison of nationalities.
(3) a scale of attitude toward war.

On April 29 the motion picture "Four Sons" was shown at a special matinée performance in the local theater. The three schedules were given again in the school the following morning, April 30.

The scale of attitude toward the Germans had the following directions and statements. The scale values, which are given here, were not, of course, given on the form presented to the students.

[1] Peterson, Ruth C., and Thurstone, L. L., "The Effect of a Motion Picture Film on Children's Attitudes toward the Germans," *The Journal of Educational Psychology*, April, 1932, pp. 241-246.

6 MOTION PICTURES AND ATTITUDES OF CHILDREN

A STUDY OF ATTITUDE TOWARD THE GERMAN PEOPLE

Write your name here_____
Boy or girl_____Age_____Grade_____
Father born in_____ Mother born in_____
        (Name of country)   (Name of country)

This is a study of attitudes toward German people. On the other side of this page you will find a number of statements expressing different attitudes toward the Germans.

    √ Put a check mark if you agree with the statement.
    ✕ Put a cross if you disagree with the statement.

Try to indicate either agreement or disagreement for each statement. If you simply cannot decide about a statement you may mark it with a question mark.

This is not an examination. There are no right or wrong answers to these statements. This is simply a study of people's attitudes toward German people. Please indicate you own convictions by a check mark when you agree and by a cross when you disagree.

(4.6) 1. The Germans as a race are very pleasant people.
(9.1) 2. I'm prejudiced against people of German descent.
(6.4) 3. German people are no better and no worse than any other people.
(1.8) 4. I admire the German people unreservedly.
(12.3) 5. The German people are the most despicable people in the world.
(4.1) 6. Some of our best American citizens are of German descent.
(.7) 7. The German people are the finest in the world.
(10.6) 8. The German soldiers were, almost without exception, cruel and brutal.
(8.4) 9. Germans are slow and unimaginative.
(3.7) 10. The more I know about the German people the better I like them.
(11.5) 11. If Germany had been wiped out by the war the world would be better off.
(7.4) 12. I don't object to German people but I don't like the German Government.
(4.8) 13. The German people were not responsible for and did not want war.
(9.7) 14. I don't trust the Germans.
(9.1) 15. The German military officer is typical of the German people.
(9.0) 16. German parents are harsh to their children.
(11.9) 17. I hate all the Germans.
(4.0) 18. The rank and file of the German army were kindly, admirable young men.
(2.7) 19. The Germans are the most desirable class of immigrants.
(2.4) 20. I'd rather have my sister marry a German than any other foreigner.
(5.7) 21. The arrogance of the German officer is not typical of the German people.
(7.0) 22. I have no particular love nor hate for the Germans.
(10.9) 23. There is nothing about Germans that I could ever like.
(7.8) 24. I suppose Germans are all right but I've never liked them.
(3.0) 25. German home life is ideal.
(10.4) 26. The people of Germany are gluttonous, militaristic, and overbearing.
(.5) 27. Germans are superior to any other nationality.

Each individual's score was the median scale value of all the statements he indorsed.

Figure 1 presents two frequency distributions which show the effect of the film "Four Sons" on the children's attitude toward Germans, as measured by the statement scale. The mean attitude of the group before seeing the film was 5.66; after seeing the picture it was 5.28. This difference of .38 represents a change in attitude favorable to the Germans. The $P.E._D$ is .0708, and the ratio of the difference to the $P.E._D$ is 5.37. The statistical facts about the two distributions are given below.

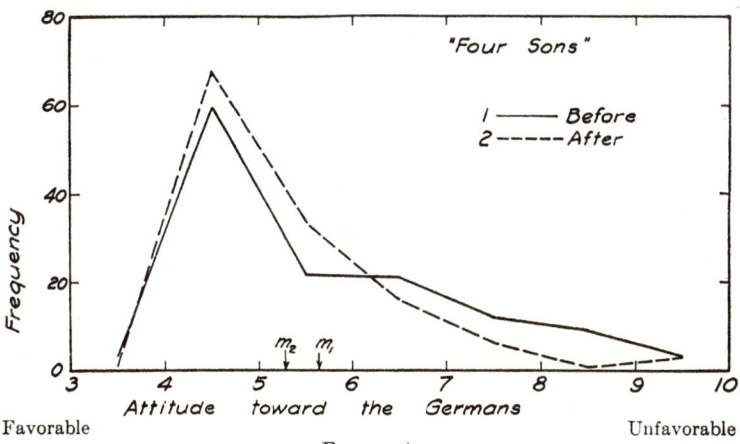

FIGURE 1
GENOA TOWNSHIP HIGH SCHOOL, GENOA, ILLINOIS
130 Children of Grades 7-12 Inclusive

$Mean_1$ (before) = 5.66	$P.E.M._1$ = .085	σ_1 = 1.43	r_{12} = .59
$Mean_2$ (after) = 5.28	$P.E.M._2$ = .066	σ_2 = 1.11	
$D_{M_1 - M_2}$ = 0.38	$P.E._D$ = .0708	$D/P.E._D$ = 5.37	

The conclusion that the film made the children definitely more favorable to the Germans seems to be justified.

The paired comparison of nationalities had the following directions:

A STUDY OF NATIONALITY PREFERENCES

Write your name here_____
Boy or girl_____Age_____Grade_____
Father born in_____ Mother born in_____
      (Name of country)   (Name of country)

This is a study of attitudes toward nationalities. You are asked to underline the one nationality of each pair that you would rather associate with. For example, the first pair is:

Englishman—Norwegian

If, in general, you prefer to associate with Englishmen rather than with Norwegians, underline *Englishman*. If you prefer, in general, to associate with Norwegians, underline *Norwegian*. If you find it difficult to decide for any pair, be sure to underline one of them anyway. If two nationalities are about equally well liked, they will have about the same number of underlinings in all of the papers. Be sure to underline one of each pair even if you have to guess.

Englishman—Norwegian   Greek—Pole
Swede—Belgian   German—Austrian
Russian—Norwegian   Irishman—German
Norwegian—Italian   Hollander—Scotchman
Norwegian—Irishman   Swede—Norwegian
Swede—Russian   Greek—Irishman
Russian—Austrian   Irishman—Frenchman
Norwegian—Spaniard   German—Norwegian

There were 15 nationalities in the list making a total of 105 comparisons of the type illustrated above.

Figure 2 shows the scale values, before and after seeing the film, for each of the nationalities which appeared in the paired comparison schedule. It is evident that the largest shift in scale value appears in the case of the Germans. It shows clearly that the film made the children more friendly toward the Germans. The shifts in scale value for the other nationalities are smaller, and most of them are of the order of magnitude which would be expected by the chance errors

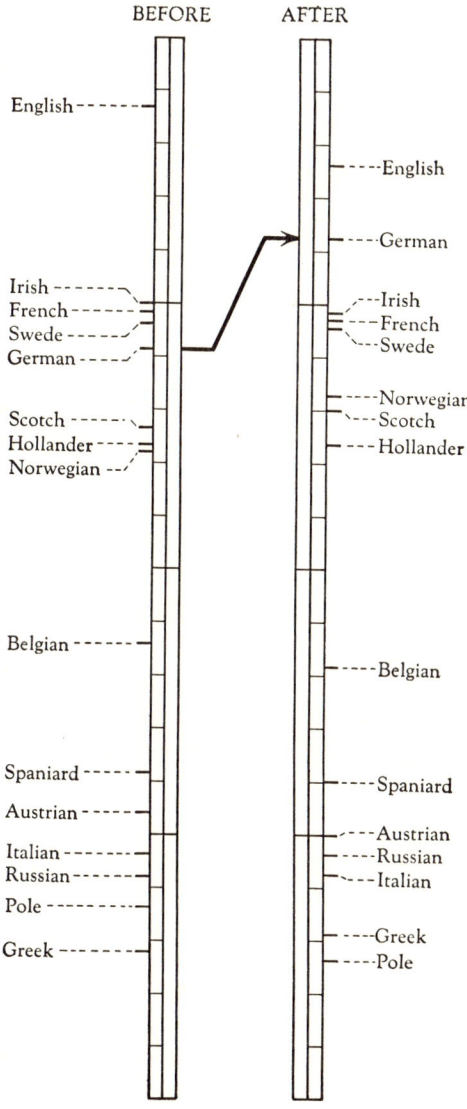

FIGURE 2
NATIONALITY PREFERENCES OF 133 SCHOOL CHILDREN IN GENOA, ILLINOIS, BEFORE AND AFTER SEEING THE FILM "FOUR SONS"

10   MOTION PICTURES AND ATTITUDES OF CHILDREN

in the proportions from which the scale values were determined.

The preferences before and after for each pair of which German was a member are tabulated below.

PAIRED COMPARISON OF NATIONALITIES

Nationality	Before	After	Difference
Pole—German	18–112	10–120	8
German—Italian	108– 22	118– 12	10
Belgian—German	38– 92	27–103	11
German—Englishman	49– 80	60– 69	11
Frenchman—German	66– 64	56– 74	10
Greek—German	22–108	10–110	2
German—Spaniard	101– 29	112– 18	11
Hollander—German	50– 80	40– 90	10
German—Austrian	105– 25	113– 17	8
Irishman—German	76– 54	63– 67	13
German—Norwegian	78– 52	81– 49	3
Scotchman—German	62– 68	57– 73	5
German—Russian	108– 22	115– 15	7
Swede—German	66– 64	53– 77	13

In every one of the above comparisons there was a change in attitude favorable to the Germans as a result of the film "Four Sons." The effect of the film on attitude is here very clearly shown. It is interesting to note that the Germans gained most (in number of shifts) at the expense of the Swedes and of the Irish.

"Four Sons" and war

Attitude toward war was measured by the following scale. (The scale values did not appear on the form given to the students.)

AN EXPERIMENTAL STUDY OF ATTITUDE TOWARD WAR

Write your name here_____
Boy or girl_____Age_____Grade_____
Father born in_____ Mother born in_____
               (Name of country)   (Name of country)

This is a study of attitudes toward war. On the following pages you will find a number of statements expressing different attitudes toward war.

    √ Put a check mark if you agree with the statement.
    × Put a cross if you disagree with the statement.

Try to indicate either agreement or disagreement for each statement. If you simply cannot decide about a statement you may mark it with a question mark.
This is not an examination. There are no right or wrong answers to these statements. This is simply a study of people's attitudes toward war. Please indicate your own convictions by a check mark when you agree and by a cross when you disagree.

(7.9) 1. Wars often right tremendous wrongs.
(1.2) 2. War appeals only to the basest of human motives and brings out all that is brutal in humanity.
(5.6) 3. Defense is the only justification for war.
(2.0) 4 War maims and kills the finest of the nation's manhood, leaving the physically unfit as a basis for coming generations.
(4.0) 5. It is almost impossible to have a large military force without being tempted to use it.
(5.6) 6. Peace and war are both essential to progress.
(8.6) 7. The abolition of war might result, through the loss of fighting energy, in the fall of civilization.
(2.9) 8. A host of young men entered the war in a spirit of idealism and unselfish devotion to a great cause, only to return disillusioned and cynical as to the value of ideals.
(1.5) 9. War in the modern world is as needless as it is suicidal.
(.4) 10. All nations should disarm immediately.
(2.3) 11. War brings misery to millions who have no voice in its declaration.
(9.0) 12. Militarism is necessary for the proper defense and protection of the individuals of a country.
(9.7) 13. A country cannot amount to much without a national honor, and war is the only means of preserving it.
(4.0) 14. An organization of all nations is imperative to establish peace.
(.3) 15. There is no conceivable justification for war.
(6.6.) 16. We should have a moderate amount of military training in our schools.
(5.8) 17. Wars are justifiable only when waged in defense of weaker nations.
(1.9) 18. In an aggressive war, the individual citizen should refuse to answer the call to arms.
(3.6) 19. No scheme of aggression or conquest can be pursued for any considerable length of time without enfeebling victor as well as vanquished.
(10.5) 20. Might is right.
(5.2) 21. Only in a war in which moral issues are clearly at stake is the individual under obligation to serve.
(7.4) 22. Until an equivalent discipline is organized, war must have its own way.
(6.8) 23. Because right may be more important than peace, war may be the lesser of two evils.
(10.0) 24. War is ennobling and stimulating of the highest and best qualities of humankind.
(.9) 25. The war makers should be jailed, and we should honor the heroes of peace.
(9.5) 26. War is the tonic of races.
(5.0) 27. Peace will come spontaneously without any effort on our part.
(9.2) 28. In the supreme offer of his life on the battle-field, a man attains to the greatest heights of glory.

(8.3) 29. The benefits of war outweigh its attendant evils.
(4.7) 30. Nations should agree not to intervene with military force in purely commercial or financial disputes.
(5.4) 31. The most that we can hope to accomplish is the partial elimination of war.
(7.8) 32. If a man's country enters a war which he does not consider justified, he should, nevertheless, serve at the front or wherever he is needed
(.4) 33. He who refuses to fight is a true hero of war.
(.3) 34. It is the moral duty of the individual to refuse to participate in any way in any war, no matter what the cause.
(3.4) 35. Civil and national differences can be settled without war.
(2.6) 36. The disrespect for human life and rights involved in war is a cause of crime waves.
(4.5) 37. The evils of war are slightly greater than its benefits.
(8.5) 38. When war is declared, we must enlist.
(1.6) 39. It is difficult to imagine any situation in which we should be justified in sanctioning or participating in another war.
(6.9) 40. It is our duty to serve in a defensive war.
(6.2) 41. Those military units should be retained which afford training to the body and mind.
(10.4) 42. There is no progress without war.
(.6) 43. Persons should pledge themselves never to aid any future war.
(3.2) 44. The misery and suffering of war are not worth its benefits.

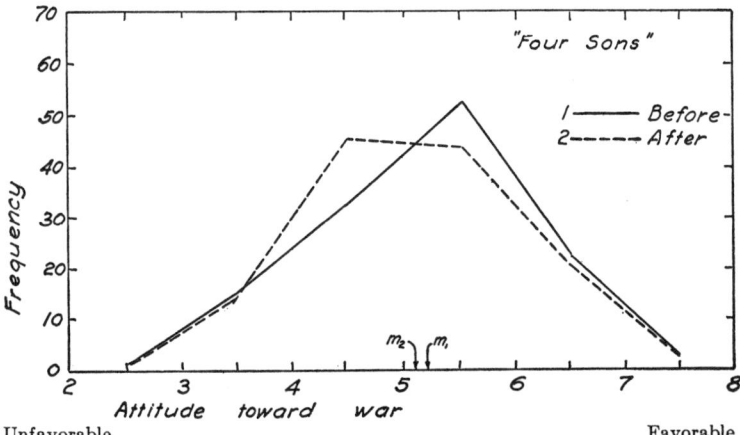

FIGURE 3

GENOA TOWNSHIP HIGH SCHOOL, GENOA, ILLINOIS
132 Children of Grades 7–12 Inclusive

Mean_1 (before) = 5.19
Mean_2 (after) = 5.10
$D_{M_1 - M_2}$ = 0.09

Figure 3 shows the distributions of attitude toward war before and after seeing the film "Four Sons." The mean score of the group before was 5.19, after 5.10. The change is not large but it is in the expected direction.

In conclusion we may say that the film "Four Sons" made the children more favorable to the Germans and slightly less favorable to war.

"Street of Chance" and gambling

An experiment was conducted in Mendota, Illinois, a town with a population of about 4,000, to study the effect of the motion picture "Street of Chance" on the children's attitudes toward gambling.[2] The experimental group consisted of 240 children in grades nine to twelve inclusive in Mendota Township High School, of which Mr. M. E. Steele is principal. A paired comparison of minor crimes was given in the school on May 15, 1930. The paired comparison schedule had the following instructions:

A STUDY OF ATTITUDE TOWARD CRIME

Write your name here_____

Boy or girl_____Age_____Grade_____

This is a study of attitudes toward crime. You are asked to underline the one crime of each pair that you think should be punished most severely. For example, the first is:

speeder—pickpocket

If, in general, you think a speeder should be punished more severely than a pickpocket, underline *speeder*. If you think a pickpocket should be punished more severely than a speeder, underline *pickpocket*. If you find it difficult to decide for any pair be sure to underline one of them, even if you have to guess.

speeder—pickpocket   bank robber—gambler
gambler—bootlegger   pickpocket—drunkard
drunkard—beggar   quack doctor—bootlegger
gangster—tramp   beggar—gangster

[2] Thurstone, L. L., "Influence of Motion Picture on Children's Attitudes," *The Journal of Social Psychology*, August, 1931, pp. 291-305.

The schedule contained 78 comparisons of the type indicated. There were 13 crimes, and each crime was paired with every other.

On May 22 the film "Street of Chance" was shown at a special matinée performance in the local theater. This film depicts the life of a gambler in such a way that the children's attitudes toward gambling might be affected. The paired comparison schedule was given again in the school the following morning, May 23.

The scale values were calculated for each crime before and after the children saw the film. Figure 4 presents the results graphically. It is evident that the scale values did not change markedly except for "gambler" which the children regarded as much worse after seeing the film.

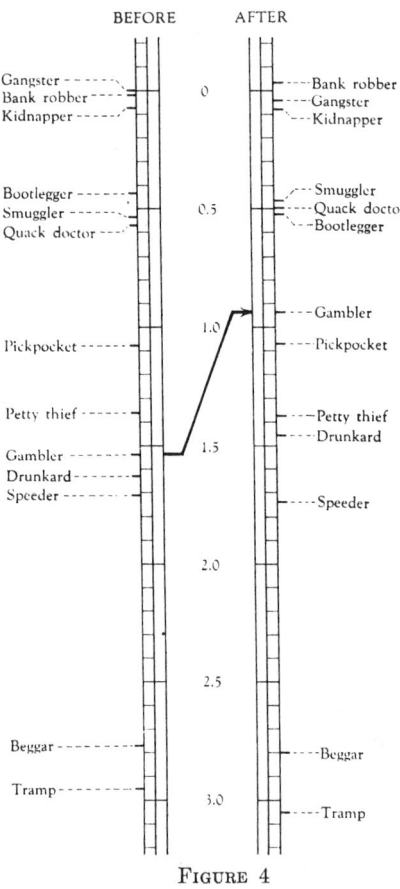

FIGURE 4

The film "Street of Chance" may be said to have a socially approved effect, since it made the children more severe in their judgment of gambling even though the gambler was an interesting, likeable character in the film.

"Hide Out" and prohibition

In Princeton, Illinois, a town of approximately 4,700 people, the experimental group consisted of 254 children in grades nine to twelve inclusive.[3] Mr. O. V. Shaffer, principal of the Princeton Township High School, assisted us in the experiment. The same paired comparison of minor crimes that was given in Mendota and a scale of attitude toward prohibition was given in the Princeton High School on May 19, 1929. The scale of attitude toward prohibition contained the following directions and statements (the scale values did not appear on the form given to the students):

A STUDY OF ATTITUDE TOWARD PROHIBITION

Write your name here_____.
Boy or girl_____Age_____Grade_____

This is a study of attitude toward Prohibition. On the other side of this page you will find a number of statements expressing different attitudes toward Prohibition.

    √   Put a check mark if you agree with the statement.
    ×   Put a cross if you disagree with the statement.

Try to indicate either agreement or disagreement for each statement. If you simply cannot decide about a statement you may mark it with a question mark.

This is not an examination. There are no right or wrong answers to these statements. This is simply a study of people's attitudes toward Prohibition. Please indicate your own convictions by a check mark when you agree and by a cross when you disagree.

(5.5)   1. It is absolutely immaterial whether we have prohibition or not.
(8.6)   2. The Eighteenth Amendment should be repealed and local option adopted.
(6.4)   3. Prohibition should come as the result of education, not legislation.
(.8)   4. The entire state and national resources should be mobilized for prohibition enforcement.
(8.2)   5. Liquor should be sold by licensed liquor dealers in restricted amounts.

[3] Thurstone, L. L., "Influence of Motion Pictures on Children's Attitudes," *The Journal of Social Psychology*, August, 1931, pp. 291-305.

(.4)	6.	Prohibition should be retained at all costs.
(9.3)	7.	Prohibition is undesirable because it drives the liquor traffic underground rather than eliminates it.
(1.4)	8.	Possession of intoxicating liquor in any form should subject individuals to punishment.
(9.2)	9.	Prohibition should be a matter to be decided by the individual, and not by the government.
(3.5)	10.	The present prohibition laws are necessary for the good of the United States.
(7.5)	11.	Manufacture of wines and beer in the home should be permitted.
(10.4)	12.	The open saloon system should be universally permitted.
(6.9)	13.	Prohibition is not desirable now because there is not a sufficiently large majority in favor of it to make enforcement effective.
(5.6)	14.	Both good and bad results have come from the Eighteenth Amendment.
(10.2)	15.	Prohibition has been tried and has proved a miserable failure.
(3.7)	16.	While the Eighteenth Amendment is a part of the constitution it should be observed.
(7.0)	17.	Prohibition is good in principle but it is doing more harm than good because it cannot be enforced.
(10.2)	18.	The Eighteenth Amendment should be repealed.
(2.5)	19.	Prohibition prevents many accidents and should, therefore, be enforced.
(4.6)	20.	It must be admitted that the Eighteenth Amendment is a restriction of personal liberty, but it has benefited many people.
(3.2)	21.	The national government should increase its appropriation for prohibition enforcement.
(4.4)	22.	Although not completely satisfactory, the present prohibition is preferable to no prohibition.
(3.3)	23.	The restriction of personal liberty under prohibition is entirely justified by the benefits.
(4.5)	24.	The experiment of prohibition may prove to have some value and may, therefore, be worth trying.
(7.8)	25.	Prohibition is an infringement upon personal liberty.
(2.4)	26.	The effect of prohibition on the national life of America is more than constructive.
(2.3)	27.	The present prohibition laws are satisfactory and their enforcement should be more severe.
(1.8)	28.	Since the liquor traffic is a curse to the human family it must be dealt with by law.

On May 26, 1929, the film "Hide Out," which portrays the experiences of a college bootlegger, was given at a special matinée performance in the local theater. The experiment had been planned with another film, which, it was found, had already been shown in Princeton. The film "Hide Out" had been criticized for its portrayal of a college bootlegger, and it was conceivable that it might affect the children's attitudes toward bootlegging and toward prohibition.

The frequency distributions of the attitudes of the group toward prohibition are shown in Figure 5. The mean attitude score of the group before and after seeing the film shows no change.

The paired comparison schedule shows only slight variations which are due to the chance fluctuations in the experimental proportions. We conclude that the film "Hide Out" had no measurable effect on the children's attitudes toward prohibition or bootlegging.

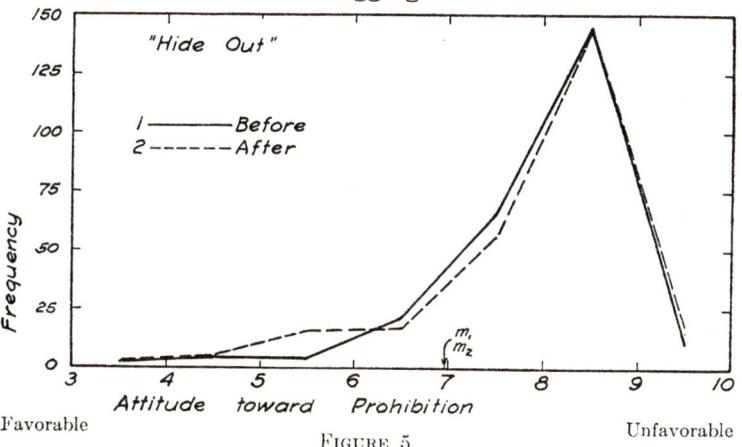

FIGURE 5

PRINCETON TOWNSHIP HIGH SCHOOL, PRINCETON, ILLINOIS
254 Children of Grades 9–12 Inclusive

Mean_1 (before) = 6.96
Mean_2 (after) = 6.97
$D_{M_1 - M_2}$ = -.01

"Son of the Gods," "Welcome Danger," and the Chinese

The two following experiments were conducted in neighboring towns of comparable populations.[4] The effect of

[4] Thurstone, L. L., "The Measurement of Change in Social Attitude," *The Journal of Social Psychology*, May, 1931, pp. 230–235.

a motion picture on the children's attitudes toward the Chinese was studied in each group, in one case with a film which has been considered friendly toward Chinese culture and in the second with a film which has been considered unfriendly and has, as such, been criticized by the Chinese themselves.

In Geneva, Illinois, a town of about 4,600 people, the following scale of attitudes toward the Chinese was given in the school on May 19, 1930, with the coöperation of Mr. H. M. Coultrap, superintendent of schools. (The scale values, which are given here, did not appear on the form used in the experiments.)

A STUDY OF ATTITUDE TOWARD THE CHINESE

Write your name here_____
Boy or girl_____Age_____Grade_____
Father born in_____ Mother born in_____
           (Name of country)   (Name of country)

This is a study of attitudes toward the Chinese. On the other side of this page you will find a number of statements expressing different attitudes toward the Chinese.

        √ Put a check mark if you agree with the statement.
        × Put a cross if you disagree with the statement.

Try to indicate either agreement or disagreement for each statement. If you simply cannot decide about a statement you may mark it with a question mark.

This is not an examination. There are no right or wrong answers to these statements. This is simply a study of people's attitudes toward the Chinese. Please indicate your own convictions by a check mark when you agree and by a cross when you disagree.

(6.5)   1. I have no particular love nor hate for the Chinese.
(10.1)   2. I dislike the Chinese more every time I see one.
(4.7)   3. The Chinese are pretty decent.
(7.2)   4. Some Chinese traits are admirable but on the whole I don't like them.
(.5)   5. The Chinese are superior to all other races.
(8.7)   6. The Chinese as part of the yellow race are inferior to the white race.
(3.5)   7. I like the Chinese.
(2.8)   8. The more I know about the Chinese the better I like them.
(11.0)   9. The Chinese are aptly described by the term "yellow devils."
(1.8) 10. The high class Chinese are superior to us.
(5.2) 11. The Chinese are different but not inferior.
(11.5) 12. I hate the Chinese.
(4.1) 13. Chinese parents are unusually devoted to their children.

The Effect of Single Pictures

(7.7) 14. Although I respect some of their qualities, I could never consider a Chinese as my friend.
(1.2) 15. I would rather live in China than any other place in the world.
(9.7) 16. There are no refined nor cultured Chinese.
(6.0) 17. The Chinese are no better and no worse than any other people.
(8.4) 18. I think Chinese should be kept out of the United States.
(2.2) 19. I consider it a privilege to associate with Chinese people.
(10.6) 20. The Chinese are inferior in every way.
(9.4) 21. I don't see how anyone could ever like the Chinese.
(3.0) 22. Chinese have a very high sense of honor.
(8.6) 23. I have no desire to know any Chinese.
(1.4) 24. Chinese people have a refinement and depth of feeling that you don't find anywhere else.
(9.8) 25. There is nothing about the Chinese that I like or admire.
(3.9) 26. I'd like to know more Chinese people.

The experimental group included 230 students in grades nine to twelve inclusive. On May 26 tickets were distributed

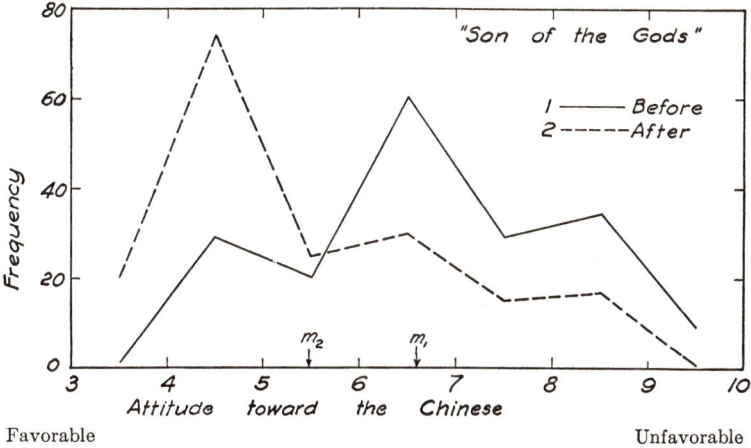

FIGURE 6
GENEVA HIGH SCHOOL, GENEVA, ILLINOIS
182 Children of Grades 9-12 Inclusive

Mean$_1$ (before) = 6.72   P.E.M.$_1$ = .073 σ_1 = 1.46 r_{12} = .57
Mean$_2$ (after) = 5.50   P.E.M.$_2$ = .077 σ_2 = 1.54
$D_{M_1 - M_2}$ = 1.22   P.E.$_D$ = .0698   D/P.E.$_D$ = 17.5

at the school which admitted the children to the regular evening performance of "Son of the Gods." "Son of the Gods" tells the story of Sam Lee who was brought up by an admirable Chinaman, Lee Ying, who Sam Lee believed was his father. Sam Lee is an attractive, able person whom people like and admire but who is not quite accepted because he is Chinese. The interpretation of Chinese life and culture is friendly, and the Chinese characters are admirable people.

On the following morning the attitude scale was given again in the school.

Figure 6 shows the two distributions of attitude toward the Chinese before and after the children saw the film. The shift in attitude is very striking. The statistical facts about the two distributions are given in the diagram on page 19.

The difference in mean attitude scores before and after seeing the film is seventeen and one-half times the probable error of the difference. The conclusion that the film "Son of the Gods" made the children more favorable toward the Chinese is undoubtedly justified.

In West Chicago, Illinois, which has a population of about 3,400, the same scale of attitude toward the Chinese was given on the same day, May 19, 1930. "Welcome Danger" is a film filled with Harold Lloyd comedy but picturing the Tong conspirators and the lawless element of underground Chinatown and has been criticized as unfriendly toward the Chinese. It was shown in the school auditorium on May 26 by permission of Mr. C. C. Byerly, principal.

The attitude scale was repeated the morning of May 27. The experimental group included 225 children in grades nine to twelve inclusive.

Figure 7 gives the two frequency distributions representing the attitudes of the group before and after seeing the motion picture. The mean score before was 5.71; after,

5.88, a change of .17 scale step, which is not large but is in the expected direction. The statistical facts about the two distributions appear below the diagram.

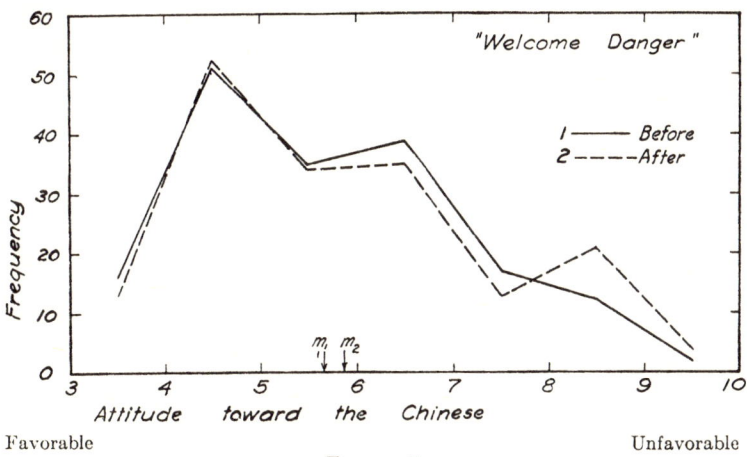

Favorable   Unfavorable

FIGURE 7
WEST CHICAGO HIGH SCHOOL, WEST CHICAGO, ILLINOIS
172 Children of Grades 9-12 Inclusive

Mean₁ (before) = 5.71   P.E.M.₁ = .073 σ_1 = 1.42 r_{12} = .58
Mean₂ (after) = 5.88   P.E.M.₂ = .080 σ_2 = 1.55
$D_{M_1 - M_2}$ = 0.17   P.E.$_D$ = .0703   D/P.E.$_D$ = 2.42

"*The Valiant*" *and capital punishment*

An experiment was conducted at Geneseo, Illinois, to study the effect of the motion picture "The Valiant" on the children's attitudes toward capital punishment. The experiment was made possible through the help of Mr. James D. Darnall, principal of Geneseo Township High School. Geneseo is a town with a population of 3,400. The experimental group consisted of 501 children in grades four to twelve inclusive. A large age range was included because we were interested in studying the differences in the effect of a motion picture on different age-groups.

"The Valiant" depicts the story of a young man who gives himself up to the police and confesses a murder. He is sentenced to die and keeps his identity a secret. His sister, whom he has not seen for many years, comes to see him. He tells her that he knew her brother who died on the field of battle. He sends her away without revealing himself as her brother and goes to his death.

The scale of attitude toward capital punishment was given in the school on January 21, 1931. "The Valiant" was shown in the local theater on February 4, and the attitude scale was given again the morning of February 5.

The scale of attitude toward capital punishment contained the following instructions and statements (the scale values were not given on the experimental scale):

A STUDY OF ATTITUDE TOWARD CAPITAL PUNISHMENT

Write your name here_____
Boy or girl_____Age_____Grade_____

This is a study of attitude toward Capital Punishment. On the other side of this page you will find a number of statements expressing different attitudes toward Capital Punishment.

    ✓ Put a check mark if you agree with the statement.
    ✗ Put a cross if you disagree with the statement.

Try to indicate either agreement or disagreement for each statement. If you simply cannot decide about a statement you may mark it with a question mark.

This is not an examination. There are no right or wrong answers to these statements. This is simply a study of people's attitudes toward Capital Punishment. Please indicate your own convictions by a check mark when you agree and by a cross when you disagree.

(7.2)   1. Capital punishment may be wrong but it is the best preventative to crime.
(0.0)   2. Capital punishment is absolutely never justified.
(6.2)   3. I think capital punishment is necessary but I wish it were not.
(10.4)   4. Any person, man or woman, young or old, who commits murder, should pay with his own life.
(2.4)   5. Capital punishment cannot be regarded as a sane method of dealing with crime.
(6.2)   6. Capital punishment is wrong but it is necessary in our imperfect civilization.
(11.0)   7. Every criminal should be executed.

The Effect of Single Pictures

(2.7) 8. Capital punishment has never been effective in preventing crime.
(5.4) 9. I don't believe in capital punishment but I'm not sure it isn't necessary.
(8.5) 10. We must have capital punishment for some crimes.
(3.9) 11. I think the return of the whipping post would be more effective than capital punishment.
(0.1) 12. I do not believe in capital punishment under any circumstances.
(3.0) 13. Capital punishment is not necessary in modern civilization.
(1.5) 14. We can't call ourselves civilized as long as we have capital punishment.
(3.4) 15. Life imprisonment is more effective than capital punishment.
(0.9) 16. Execution of criminals is a disgrace to civilized society.
(9.6) 17. Capital punishment is just and necessary.
(5.8) 18. I do not believe in capital punishment but it is not practically advisable to abolish it.
(0.6) 19. Capital punishment is the most hideous practice of our time.
(9.4) 20. Capital punishment gives the criminal what he deserves.
(2.0) 21. The state cannot teach the sacredness of human life by destroying it.
(5.5) 22. It doesn't make any difference to me whether we have capital punishment or not.
(7.9) 23. Capital punishment is justified only for premeditated murder.
(9.1) 24. Capital punishment should be used more often than it is.

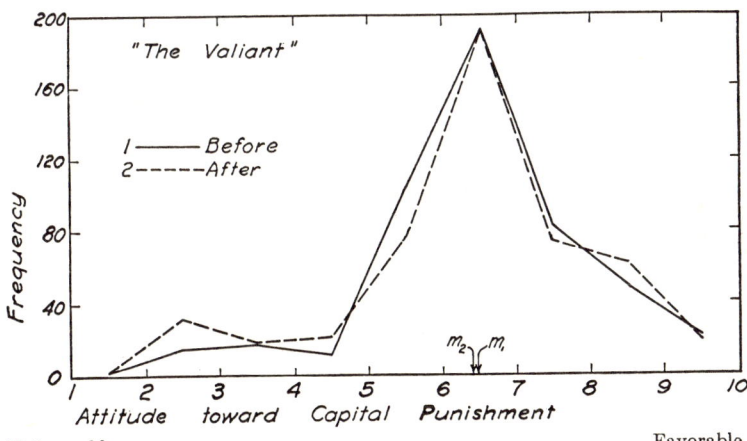

Figure 8

Geneseo Township High School, Geneseo, Illinois
501 Children of Grades 4–12 Inclusive

Mean_1 (before) = 6.46 P.E.M._1 = .046 σ_1 = 1.52 r_{12} = .71
Mean_2 (after) = 6.41 P.E.M._2 = .051 σ_2 = 1.70
$D_{M_1 - M_2}$ = .05 P.E._D = .037 $D/\text{P.E.}_D$ = 1.35

The two frequency distributions, representing the attitudes of the children before and after seeing the film are given in Figure 8. The mean score of the group before was 6.46, after 6.41, a change of .05 scale step with a $P.E._D$ of .037. The ratio of the difference to the $P.E._D$ is 1.35 which, although it is not a significant difference, is in the expected direction.

We conclude that, although the film "The Valiant" showed a slight effect on the children's attitudes, making them less favorable to capital punishment, the effect is not statistically significant. Neither the mean attitude scores nor the amount of change showed any consistent variation from the younger to the older age groups.

"Journey's End" and war

Mr. H. C. Storm, superintendent of schools at Batavia, Illinois, helped us arrange an experiment in his school to study the effect of the film "Journey's End" on the children's attitudes toward war. Batavia is a town of about 5,000 people. Three hundred one children in grades seven to twelve took part in the experiment.

A scale of attitude toward war was given in the school on January 30, 1931. The motion picture "Journey's End" was shown at a special matinée performance on February 24, and the attitude scale was given again on February 25.

The scale of attitude toward war was as follows. (The scale values were not given on the experimental form.)

A STUDY OF ATTITUDE TOWARD WAR

Write your name here_____
Boy or girl_____ Age_____ Grade_____
Father born in_____ Mother born in_____
   (Name of country)   (Name of country)

This is a study of attitude toward war. On the other side of this page you will find a number of statements expressing different attitudes toward war.

  √ Put a check mark if you agree with the statement.
  × Put a cross if you disagree with that statement.

Try to indicate either agreement or disagreement for each statement. If you simply cannot decide about a statement you may mark it with a question mark.

This is not an examination. There are no right or wrong answers to these statements. This is simply a study of people's attitudes toward war. Please indicate your own convictions by a check mark when you agree and by a cross when you disagree.

(4.2)   1. War is hardly necessary in the modern world.
(1.4)   2. War is a futile struggle resulting in self-destruction.
(8.3)   3. The desirable results of war have not received the attention they deserve.
(3.3)   4. A host of young men returned from the war disillusioned and cynical.
(7.0)   5. Another war would be terrible but it might be worth the price.
(11.0)   6. War is glorious.
(7.8)   7. War is sometimes necessary because right is more important than peace.
(2.1)   8. War destroys the finest of the nation's manhood.
(4.6)   9. We want no more war if it can be avoided without dishonor.
(9.5) 10. High idealism is born in war.
(6.6) 11. There are some arguments in favor of war.
(3.0) 12. There will be no more wars when people become really civilized.
(0.0) 13. Every last one of us should refuse to take part in any way in any war.
(5.5) 14. It is hard to decide whether wars do more harm than good.
(2.4) 15. War is an unnecessary waste of human life.
(6.3) 16. Peace and war are both essential to progress.
(0.4) 17. War should be avoided at any cost.
(7.5) 18. Under some conditions, war is necessary to maintain justice.
(9.2) 19. War develops the moral strength of men.
(3.2) 20. The benefits of war are not worth its misery and suffering.
(10.8) 21. The highest duty of man is to fight for the power and glory of his nation.
(1.6) 22. War in the modern world is as needless as it is terrible.
(8.8) 23. Every man should enlist as soon as war is declared.
(0.2) 24. There is no conceivable justification for war.
(5.4) 25. War brings out both good and bad qualities in men.
(10.1) 26. There can be no progress without war.
(3.7) 27. International disputes should be settled without war.
(2.2) 28. The soldier suffers terribly and gains nothing.
(0.7) 29. War is simply murder sanctioned by governments.
(8.5) 30. War is a satisfactory way to solve international difficulties.
(6.0) 31. War has some benefits; but it's a big price to pay for them.
(9.8) 32. War stimulates men to their noblest efforts.

Figure 9 represents the distributions of attitude of the group before and after seeing the picture. The change in attitude is very small, but it is in the expected direction.

The comparison of the effect of "Journey's End" and "All Quiet on the Western Front." both of which are considered outstanding pictures and powerful as anti-war propaganda, is interesting. Next in this report we shall present the results of an experiment using the picture "All Quiet on the Western Front." In that experiment the change in attitude is very striking. There is nothing in the experimental set-up which might explain the difference, and we consider it probable that the picture "Journey's End" is too sophisticated in its propaganda for high school children. It is possible that the two pictures might have more nearly equal effects on the attitudes of adults.

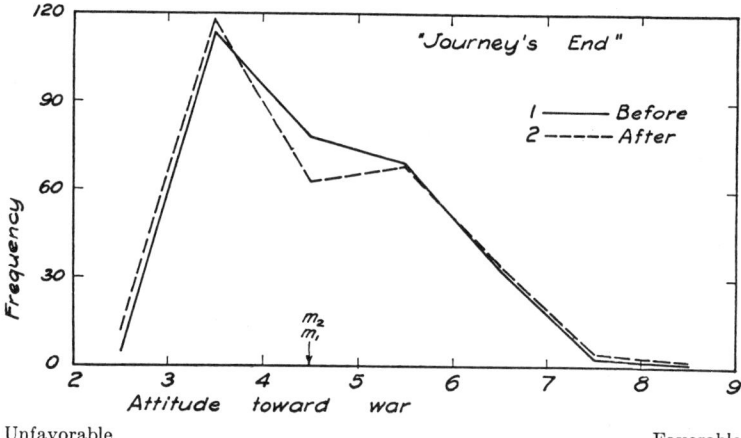

FIGURE 9
BATAVIA HIGH SCHOOL, BATAVIA, ILLINOIS
301 Children of Grades 7–12 Inclusive

Mean_1 (before) = 4.52 P.E.M._1 = .042 $\sigma_1 = 1.08$ $r_{12} = .63$
Mean_2 (after) = 4.48 P.E.M._2 = .047 $\sigma_2 = 1.20$
$D_{M_1 - M_2}$ = .04 P.E._D = .0384 $D/\text{P.E.}_D = 1.04$

"All Quiet on the Western Front" and war

The motion picture "All Quiet on the Western Front" was shown to 214 high school students in Paxton, Illinois (population, 3,000), to study the effect of the film on attitude toward war. Mr. John J. Swinney, principal of the Paxton Community High School, arranged to have the scale of attitude toward war given in his school on March 16, 1931. The picture was shown in the local theater on March 25, and the attitude scale was given in the school on March 26.

The attitude scale used in this experiment was the same as the scale used in the experiment at Batavia, Illinois.

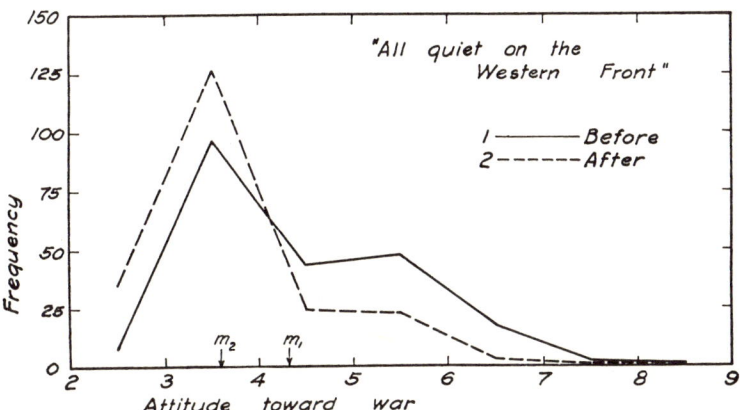

FIGURE 10

PAXTON COMMUNITY HIGH SCHOOL, PAXTON, ILLINOIS
214 Children of Grades 9–12 Inclusive

Mean_1 (before) = 4.33 $P.E.M._1$ = .052 σ_1 = 1.12 r_{12} = .57
Mean_2 (after)   = 3.65 $P.E.M._2$ = .046 σ_2 = 0.99
$D_{M_1 - M_2}$ = .68 $P.E._D$ = .0454 $D/P.E._D$ = 14.98

In Figure 10 we have plotted the frequency distributions of the scores on attitude toward war before and after seeing the film. The mean attitude of the group before was 4.33; after seeing the picture it was 3.65, a change of .68 of a scale step. The change is in the direction of pacifism. The $P.E._D$ is 0.454, the ratio of the difference to the $P.E._D$ is 14.98.

The change in the children's attitude toward war as a result of seeing the film "All Quiet on the Western Front" is very evident.

"The Criminal Code" and punishment of criminals

The motion picture "The Criminal Code" was used in experiments at Watseka (population 3,100) and in Galesburg, Illinois (population 28,800). In Watseka the experimental group included 276 children in grades seven to twelve; the Galesburg group included 246 students of Knox College. We wished to study the difference in the effect of this picture on high school and on college students.

Mr. E. W. Powers, principal of the Watseka Community High School, suggested that the scale of attitude toward the punishment of criminals which was used in the experiment should be simplified. He felt that some of the statements in the original form might not be easily understood by the group, especially the seventh and eighth grades. Consequently, the statements were given in the following form:

A STUDY OF ATTITUDE TOWARD PUNISHMENT OF CRIMINALS

Write your name here_____
Boy or gir_____ Age_____ Grade_____

This is a study of attitudes toward punishment of criminals. On the other side of this page you will find a number of statements expressing different attitudes toward punishment of criminals.

√ Put a check mark if you agree with the statement.
× Put a cross if you disagree with the statement.

Try to indicate either agreement or disagreement for each statement. If you simply cannot decide about a statement you may mark it with a question mark.

This is not an examination. There are no right or wrong answers to these statements. This is simply a study of people's attitudes toward the punishment of criminals. Please indicate your own convictions by a check mark when you agree and by a cross when you disagree.

(5.8) 1. A person should be put in prison only for very bad crimes.
(1.1) 2. It is wrong for the government to make any people suffer in prison.

The Effect of Single Pictures

(9.0) 3. Hard prison life will keep men from committing crime.
(4.8) 4. Punishment does not make some criminals any better.
(2.7) 5. In prison many men learn to be worse criminals.
(8.2) 6. We should not bother about the comfort of a prisoner.
(8.6) 7. A criminal will go straight only when he finds that prison life is hard.
(0.5) 8. There isn't any punishment that will keep men from committing crime.
(3.1) 9. Prisons make men worse than they were.
(5.5) 10. Only men who have committed several crimes should be punished.
(10.0) 11. We should use physical punishment in dealing with all criminals.
(5.3) 12. I don't know anything about the treatment of crime.
(0.8) 13. We should be ashamed to punish criminals.
(9.3) 14. Putting a criminal in a cell by himself will make him sorry.
(4.1) 15. It is better for us to be easy on certain criminals.
(1.5) 16. Only kind treatment can cure criminals.
(3.1) 17. Cruel prison treatment makes criminals want to get even.
(9.8) 18. No kindness should be shown to prisoners.
(3.4) 19. Many men who aren't very bad become dangerous criminals after a prison term.
(8.1) 20. If we do not punish criminals, we will have more crime.
(10.6) 21. Only by very cruel punishment can we cure the criminal.
(1.8) 22. Severe punishment makes men worse criminals.
(6.4) 23. A criminal should be punished first and then reformed.
(8.8) 24. One way to keep men from crime is to make them suffer.
(2.3) 25. We cannot make a good citizen of a criminal if we punish him.
(9.2) 26. Having to live on bread and water in prison will cure the criminal.
(3.2) 27. Cruel treatment of a criminal makes him more dangerous.
(7.6) 28. A jail sentence will cure many criminals.
(10.3) 29. Prisoners should be chained.
(4.6) 30. In order to decide how to treat a criminal we should know what kind of person he is.
(0.0) 31. Even the very worst criminal should not be mistreated.
(7.4) 32. It is fair for the government to punish men who break the laws.
(2.7) 33. Kind treatment makes the criminal want to be good.
(6.6) 34. We have to use some punishment in dealing with criminals.

February 19, 1931 was the date of the first application of the scale, the motion picture was shown in a local theater on the afternoon of March 3, and the attitude scale was given in the school the second time on March 4.

The two frequency distributions, representing the attitudes of the group before and after they saw the film, are given in Figure 11 on page 30.

The mean score before was 5.30; after, 4.80, a change of 50 of a scale step. The difference is $11.7 \times P.E._D$.

The experiment conducted at Knox College, Galesburg, with the assistance of Mr. Rutledge T. Wiltbank, used the same scale of attitude toward punishment of criminals that was used in Watseka, but in its original form. It is given below.

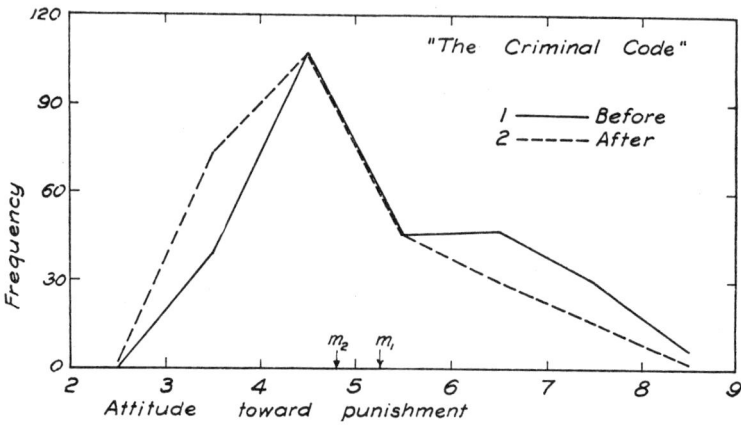

FIGURE 11
WATSEKA COMMUNITY HIGH SCHOOL, WATSEKA, ILLINOIS
276 Children of Grades 7-12 Inclusive

Mean_1 (before) = 5.30 $\text{P.E.M.}_1 = .054$ $\sigma_1 = 1.33$ $r_{12} = .66$
Mean_2 (after) = 4.80 $\text{P.E.M.}_2 = .049$ $\sigma_2 = 1.21$
$D_{M_1 - M_2}$ = .50 $\text{P.E.}_D = .0437$ $D/\text{P.E.}_D = 11.7$

A STUDY OF ATTITUDE TOWARD PUNISHMENT OF CRIMINALS

Write your name here_____
Boy or girl_____ Age_____ Grade_____

This is a study of attitudes toward punishment of criminals. On the other side of this page you will find a number of statements expressing different attitudes toward punishment of criminals.

√ Put a check mark if you agree with the statement.
✕ Put a cross if you disagree with the statement.

Try to indicate either agreement or disagreement for each statement. If you simply cannot decide about a statement you may mark it with a question mark.

This is not an examination. There are no right or wrong answers to these statements. This is simply a study of people's attitudes toward the punishment of criminals. Please indicate your own convictions by a check mark when **you agree and by a cross when you disagree.**

The Effect of Single Pictures

(5.8) 1. A person should be imprisoned only for serious offenses.
(1.1) 2. It is wrong for society to make any of its members suffer.
(9.0) 3. Hard prison life will keep men from committing crime.
(4.8) 4. Some criminals do not benefit from punishment.
(2.7) 5. Most prisons are schools of crime.
(8.2) 6. We should not consider the comfort of a prisoner.
(8.6) 7. A criminal will go straight only when he finds that prison life is hard.
(0.5) 8. No punishment can reduce crime.
(3.1) 9. Prison influence is degenerating.
(5.5) 10. Only habitual criminals should be punished.
(10.0) 11. We should employ corporal punishment in dealing with all criminals.
(5.3) 12. I have no opinion about the treatment of crime.
(0.8) 13. Punishment of criminals is a disgrace to civilized society.
(9.3) 14. Solitary confinement will make the criminal penitent.
(4.1) 15. It is advantageous to society to spare certain criminals.
(1.5) 16. Only humane treatment can cure criminals.
(3.1) 17. Harsh imprisonment merely embitters a criminal.
(9.8) 18. No leniency should be shown to convicts.
(3.4) 19. Many petty offenders become dangerous criminals after a prison term.
(8.1) 20. Failure to punish the criminal encourages crime.
(10.6) 21. Only by extreme brutal punishment can we cure the criminal.
(1.8) 22. The more severely a man is punished, the greater criminal he becomes.
(6.4) 23. A criminal should be punished first and then reformed.
(8.8) 24. One way to deter men from crime is to make them suffer.
(2.3) 25. Punishment is wasteful of human life.
(9.2) 26. A bread and water diet in prison will cure the criminal.
(3.2) 27. Brutal treatment of a criminal makes him more dangerous.
(7.6) 28. A jail sentence will cure many criminals of further offenses.
(10.3) 29. Prison inmates should be put in irons.
(4.6) 30. We should consider the individual in treating crime.
(0.0) 31. Even the most vicious criminal should not be harmed.
(7.4) 32. It is fair for society to punish those who offend against it.
(2.7) 33. Humane treatment inspires the criminal to be good.
(6.6) 34. Some punishment is necessary in dealing with the criminal.

The attitude scale was given to the college students on February 16, 1931. "The Criminal Code" was shown at a special performance in the West Theater on Saturday morning, February 28, and the attitude scale was given in the college the following Monday, March 1st.

The two distributions, before and after, are given in Figure 12. The mean attitude of the group before seeing the film was 4.95; after, 4.46, a change of .49 scale step with a

P.E.$_D$ of .04, giving a ratio of the difference to the P.E.$_D$ of 12.2.

The change in attitude for the high school group (.50) is comparable to that for the college group (.49). The mean attitude of the high school group (5.30) before the motion picture, was, however, considerably higher than that of the college group (4.95). The effect of the motion picture on the college group, although slightly smaller than the effect on the high school group, may be equally or more signifi-

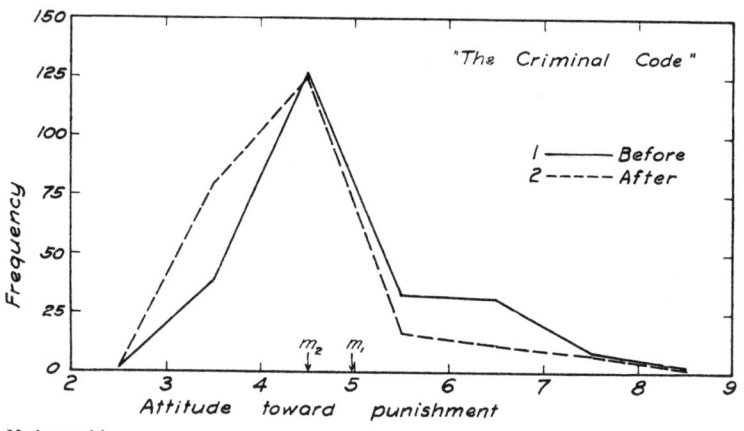

FIGURE 12
KNOX COLLEGE, GALESBURG, ILLINOIS
246 Students of Years 1–4 Inclusive

Mean$_1$ (before) = 4.95   P.E.M.$_1$ = .049 σ_1 = 1.14 r_{12} = .65
Mean$_2$ (after) = 4.46   P.E.M.$_2$ = .046 σ_2 = 1.07
$D_{M_1 - M_2}$ = .49   P.E.$_D$ = .04 $D/P.E._D$ = 12.2

cant. The college group was less in favor of punishment of criminals than the high school group was before the film was shown and changed almost as much. In other words, a change in the direction of leniency from a position which was originally more in favor of leniency may be more significant than a slightly larger change from an original position which was more in favor of punishment.

Figure 13 gives the two frequency distributions before and after seeing "The Criminal Code" for the combined groups of Galesburg and Watseka. The statistical facts about the two distributions are given below.

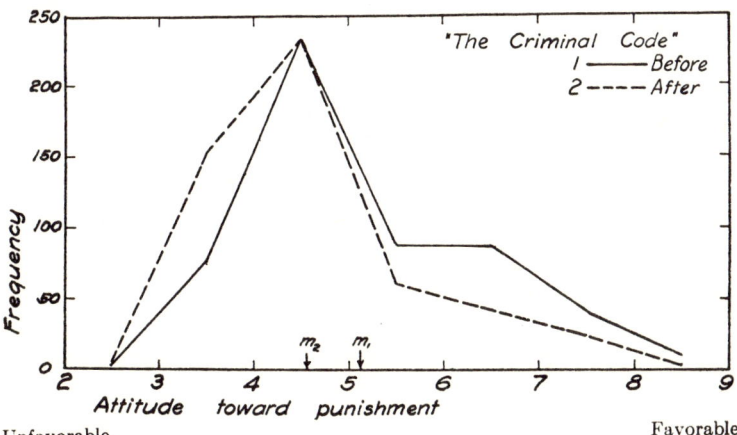

Unfavorable   Favorable

FIGURE 13

KNOX COLLEGE AND WATSEKA COMMUNITY HIGH SCHOOL
522 Students, Years 1-4 Inclusive and Grades 7-12 Inclusive

Mean₁ (before) = 5.137   P.E.M.₁ = .037 σ_1 = 1.26 r_{12} = .664
Mean₂ (after) = 4.642   P.E.M.₂ = .034 σ_2 = 1.16
$D_{M_1 - M_2}$ = .495   P.E._D = .0293   D/P.E._D = 16.9

"Alibi" and punishment of criminals

The film "Alibi" tells the story of a police sergeant's daughter who sympathizes with crooks and believes that they are persecuted by the police. The picture finally shows the girl convinced that the gangster has not reformed, and she is disillusioned about persecuted crooks. This picture has been barred by the censor board of a large city because its effect was considered anti-social. We were interested in finding out whether the film had a measurable effect on the attitudes of high school children toward the treatment of criminals.

The scale of attitude toward punishment of criminals was given to 352 students in grades seven to twelve inclusive in the Aledo, Illinios, public schools. Aledo has a population of 2,200. The experiment was carried on with the assistance of Mr. L. C. McCarty, superintendent of the Aledo public schools, and Mr. R. E. Dahl, principal of the Junior High School. The scale was given on April 27, 1931, the motion picture was shown at a local theater on May 14, and the scale was given the second time on May 15.

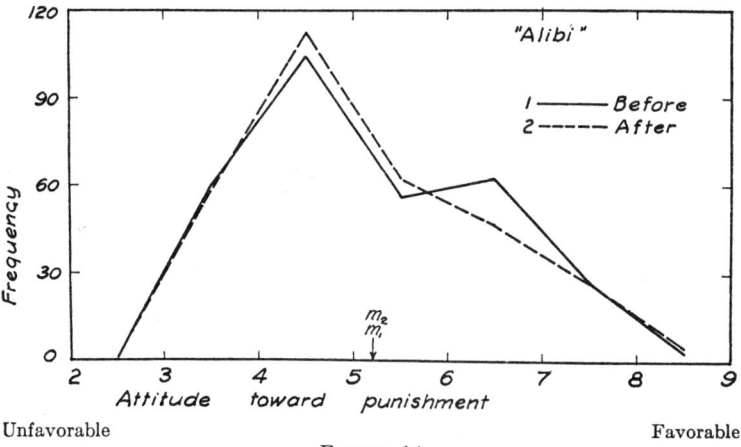

FIGURE 14
ALEDO PUBLIC SCHOOLS, ALEDO, ILLINOIS
314 Children of Grades 7–12 Inclusive

$Mean_1$ (before) = 5.24 $P.E.M._1$ = .050 σ_1 = 1.31 r_{12} = .65
$Mean_2$ (after) = 5.17 $P.E.M._2$ = .050 σ_2 = 1.31
$D_{M_1 - M_2}$ = .07 $P.E._D$ = .042 $D/P.E._D$ = 1.67

Figure 14 shows the frequency distributions of attitude before and after the children saw the film. The mean attitude of the group before was 5.24; after, 5.17, a change of .07 with a $P.E._D$ of .042, giving a ratio of the difference to the $P.E._D$ of 1.67. There was a slight change of attitude in the direction of leniency toward the punishment of criminals, but the change is not statistically significant.

We conclude, therefore, that the film "Alibi" had no measurable effect on the attitudes of the children toward punishment of criminals.

"The Birth of a Nation" and the Negro

"The Birth of a Nation," a picture very widely known a number of years ago, was returned to the screen in 1931 with sound accompaniment. It has been considered as powerful anti-Negro propaganda. We wished to study the effect of this picture on attitude toward the Negro, and with the coöperation of Mr. H. A. Dean, superintendent of schools in Crystal Lake, Illinois, a scale of attitude toward the Negro was given to 434 students in grades six to twelve inclusive in his school. Crystal Lake is a town of 3,700 people, but has no Negroes. Mr. Dean told us that, in all probability, very few of the children had known or even seen Negroes. The mean attitude of the group on the first application of the scale of attitude toward the Negro was 7.46. The range of the scale is from zero to eleven, with the higher scale values for the statements which are favorable to the Negro.

The attitude scale and the scale values for each statement are given below. (The scale values were not, of course, given on the form used.)

A STUDY OF ATTITUDE TOWARD THE NEGRO

Write your name here _____
Boy or girl _____ Age _____ Grade _____
Father born in _____ Mother born in _____
             (Name of country)   (Name of country)

This is a study of attitudes toward the Negro. On the other side of this page you will find a number of statements expressing different attitudes toward the Negro.

    √ Put a check mark if you agree with the statement.
    × Put a cross if you disagree with the statement.

Try to indicate either agreement or disagreement for each statement. If you simply cannot decide about a statement you may mark it with a question mark.

This is not an examination. There are no right or wrong answers to these statements. This is simply a study of people's attitudes toward the Negro. Please indicate your own convictions by a check mark when you agree and by a cross when you disagree.

(5.4) 1. I am not at all interested in how the Negro rates socially.
(7.3) 2. You cannot condemn the entire black race because of the actions of some of its members.
(2.7) 3. Under no circumstances should Negro children be allowed to attend the same schools as white children.
(0.8) 4. The white race must be kept pure at all costs, even if the Negroes have to be killed off.
(8.9) 5. Give the Negro time. Within the next fifty years he will astonish you.
(4.3) 6. The Negro should have freedom but should never be treated as the equal of the white man.
(1.8) 7. No person with the slightest trace of Negro blood should associate with white people or be classed as a white man.
(10.3) 8. I believe that the Negro deserves the same social privileges as the white man.
(9.6) 9. Give the Negro a high position in society and he will show himself equal to it.
(6.8) 10. In a thousand years the Negro might become the white man's equal; then his social position should be equal to the white man's.
(4.7) 11. I think the colored race should hold a somewhat lower social position than the white race.
(2.1) 12. I can stand a "nigger" in his place but I cannot stand him as the equal of the white man.
(0.9) 13. The Negro will always remain as he is—a little higher than the animals.
(10.3) 14. The Negro should be considered as equal to the white man and be given the white man's advantages.
(7.9) 15. Our refusal to accept the Negro is not based on any fact in nature but on a prejudice which should be overcome.
(6.5) 16. The courts are far more unfair to the Negro than the real differences between the races justify.
(3.2) 17. The Negro and the white man must be kept apart in all social affairs where they might be taken as equal.

The Effect of Single Pictures 37

(1.7) 18. Negroes should not be allowed to associate with white people in any way.
(9.6) 19. The white and colored races should enjoy the same privileges and protection.
(5.5) 20. The Negro problem will settle itself without our worrying about it.
(3.6) 21. The Negro should be treated and thought of as a servant for the white man.
(0.9) 22. The Negro should be considered in the lowest class among human beings.
(10.0) 23. By nature the Negro and the white man are equal.
(7.7) 24. The Negro is perfectly capable of taking care of himself, if the white man would only let him alone.

The above scale was given in the school on May 18, 1931. "The Birth of a Nation" was shown at a local theater on the afternoon of May 25 at a special performance for the

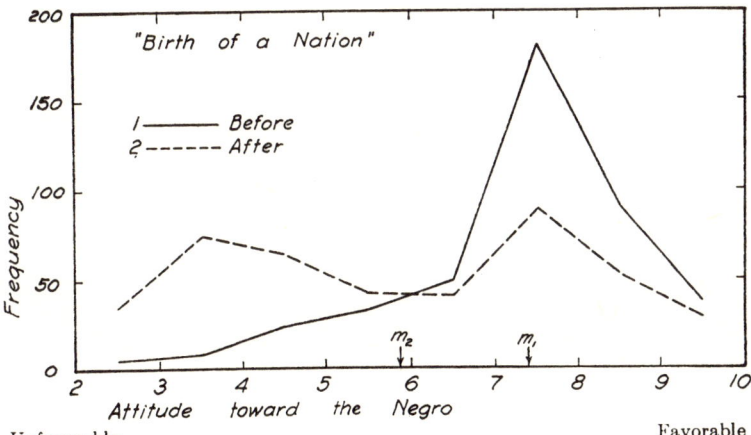

FIGURE 15
CRYSTAL LAKE HIGH SCHOOL, CRYSTAL LAKE, ILLINOIS
434 Children of Grades 6–12 Inclusive

Mean₁ (before) = 7.41   P.E.M.₁ = .046 σ_1 = 1.4 r_{12} = .55
Mean₂ (after) = 5.93   P.E.M.₂ = .070 σ_2 = 2.2
$D_{M_1 - M_2}$ = 1.48   P.E.$_D$ = .058   D/P.E.$_D$ = 25.5

experimental group. The attitude scale was given again in the school on May 26.

The two frequency distributions, representing the attitudes of the group before and after they saw the picture, are given in Figure 15. The change is very striking, the average change for the group of 434 children being 1.48 scale steps. The difference is 25.5 × $P.E._D$. This is the largest effect found in any of the experiments we conducted.

The conclusion that the motion picture "The Birth of a Nation" had the effect of making the children less favorable to the Negro is undoubtedly justified. A later section of this report will give the persistence of the effect measured. It was interesting to find that the change in attitude was so marked and that, after an interval, the attitude of the group was still definitely less favorable to the Negro than before the film was seen.

CHAPTER III

THE CUMULATIVE EFFECT OF PICTURES

Attitude toward war

A SERIES of experiments on the cumulative effect of motion pictures was conducted in Mooseheart, Illinois, during the summer of 1931. Mooseheart is a community organized and maintained by The Loyal Order of the Moose for the children of deceased members of the Order. The experiments were made possible through the interest and coöperation of Mr. Ernest N. Roselle, Superintendent of Mooseheart, Mr. Martin L. Reymert, Director of Mooseheart Laboratory for Child Research, Mr. V. A. Bird, Director of Education, and Mr. L. A. Meyer, Research Assistant. Their help was very generously given.

The experiments at Mooseheart were set up to study the cumulative effect of two or more pictures on the same issue. School sessions continue through the summer at Mooseheart, and the experiments were carried on during July and August, 1931. About 750 children in grades six to twelve inclusive were included in the experimental group. This total group was divided into five subgroups, A, B, C, D, E, including in each subgroup a cross section of the total group.

The following summary gives the set-up of the first experiment, which studied change in attitude toward war. The attitude scale used was the same as the one used in the experiments at Batavia and Paxton, Illinois (see page 24).

July 8, 1931—Grades six to twelve inclusive took the scale of attitude toward war.
July 20, 1931—Groups B and C saw "All Quiet on the Western Front."
July 21, 1931—Group B took the scale of attitude toward war. Groups C, D, and E saw "Journey's End."
July 22, 1931—Groups C, D, and A took the scale. Group E saw "All Quiet on the Western Front."
July 23, 1931—Group E took the scale.

This set-up gave the following data:

(1) Group A—Attitude score with two weeks' interval with no interposed motion picture.
(2) Group B—The effect of the film "All Quiet on the Western Front."
(3) Group C—Cumulative effect of "All Quiet on the Western Front" and "Journey's End" seen in that order.
(4) Group D—The effect of the film "Journey's End."
(5) Group E—Cumulative effect of films "Journey's End" and "All Quiet on the Western Front" seen in that order.

The table gives a résumé of the results.

Group	N	Picture	M_1	M_2	D	$P.E._D$	$D/P.E._D$
A	150	None	5.04	4.92	.12	.065	1.85
B	152	"All Quiet on the Western Front"	5.05	4.56	.49	.07	6.97
C	148	"All Quiet" and "Journey's End"	4.95	4.46	.49	.059	8.26
D	147	"Journey's End"	4.91	4.58	.33	.065	5.07
E	148	"Journey's End" and "All Quiet"	5.06	4.52	.54	.067	8.06

It may be noted that the picture "All Quiet on the Western Front" had a greater single effect than the picture "Journey's End." The group who saw "Journey's End" after they had seen "All Quiet on the Western Front" showed no greater absolute change in attitude than the group who saw only "All Quiet on the Western Front."

The Cumulative Effect of Pictures

The group who saw "Journey's End" first and "All Quiet on the Western Front" subsequently, showed the largest absolute change of attitude. If the differentiating ratios are observed, however, it is noted that groups C and E, who saw both pictures, had the most significant changes in attitude. From the above data we offer the conclusion that two films on the same issue show a cumulative effect on the children's attitude.

The diagrams below give the frequency distributions and statistical facts for each group.

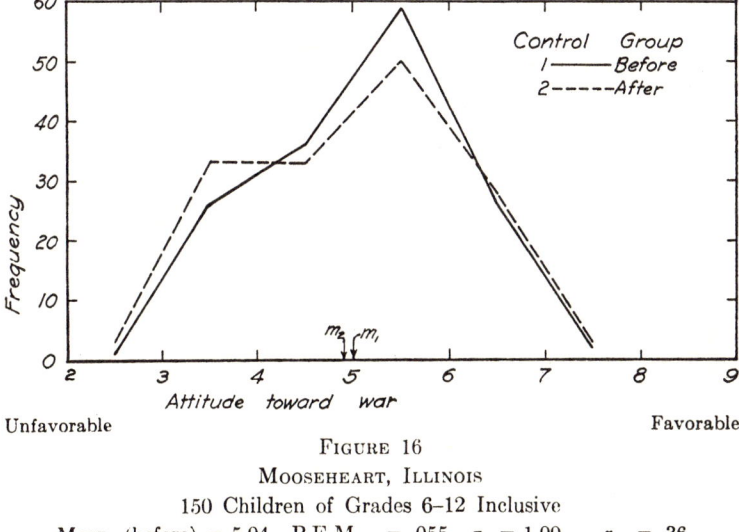

FIGURE 16
MOOSEHEART, ILLINOIS
150 Children of Grades 6–12 Inclusive

Mean$_1$ (before) = 5.04   P.E.M.$_1$ = .055 σ_1 = 1.00 r_{12} = .36
Mean$_2$ (after) = 4.92   P.E.M.$_2$ = .060 σ_2 = 1.08
$D_{M_1 - M_2}$ = .12   P.E.$_D$ = .065   D/P.E.$_D$ = 1.85

Figure 21 presents the distribution of attitude, before and after seeing the motion pictures, for the combined groups B, C, D, and E. This excludes Group A who did not see either of the pictures. The mean attitude score of this

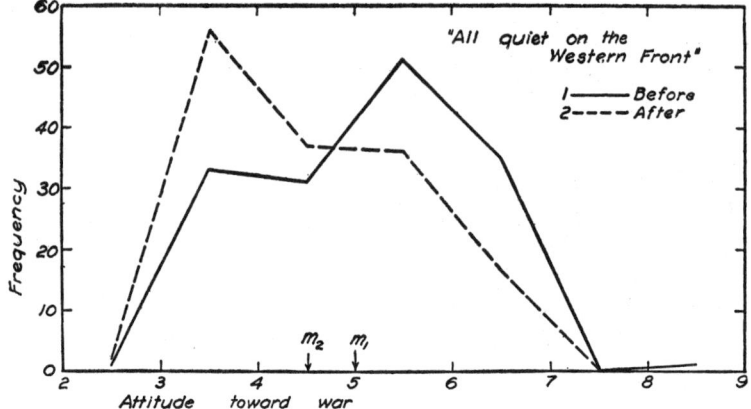

Unfavorable   FIGURE 17   Favorable

MOOSEHEART, ILLINOIS

152 Children of Grades 6–12 Inclusive

Mean_1 (before) = 5.05 P.E.M._1 = .057 $\sigma_1 = 1.05$ $r_{12} = .27$
Mean_2 (after)   = 4.56 P.E.M._2 = .059 $\sigma_2 = 1.08$
$D_{M_1 - M_2}$ = .49 P.E._D = .0703 $D/\text{P.E.}_D = 6.97$

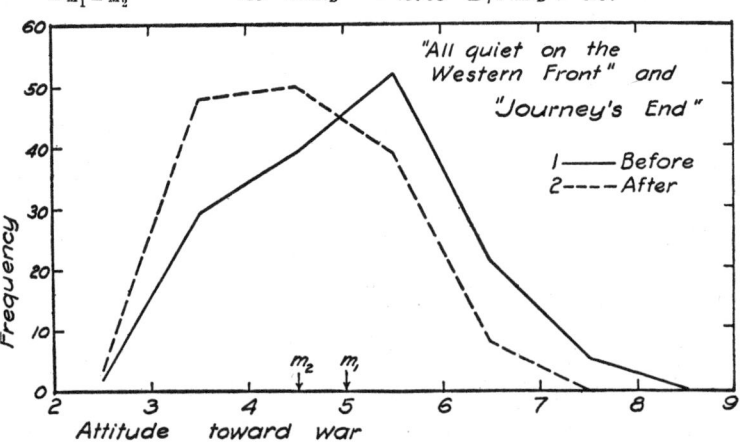

Unfavorable   FIGURE 18   Favorable

MOOSEHEART, ILLINOIS

148 Children of Grades 6–12 Inclusive

Mean_1 (before) = 4.95 P.E.M._1 = .058 $\sigma_1 = 1.04$ $r_{12} = .41$
Mean_2 (after)   = 4.46 P.E.M._2 = .051 $\sigma_2 = 0.92$
$D_{M_1 - M_2}$ = .49 P.E._D = .0593 $D/\text{P.E.}_D = 8.26$

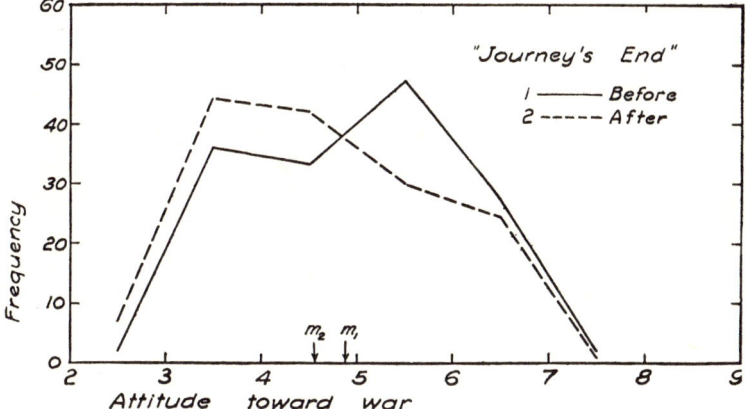

Unfavorable   FIGURE 19   Favorable

MOOSEHEART, ILLINOIS

147 Children of Grades 6–12 Inclusive

Mean$_1$ (before) = 4.91   P.E.M.$_1$ = .062 σ_1 = 1.11 r_{12} = .46
Mean$_2$ (after) = 4.58   P.E.M.$_2$ = .063 σ_2 = 1.14
$D_{M_1 - M_2}$ = .33   P.E.$_D$ = .065   D/P.E.$_D$ = 5.07

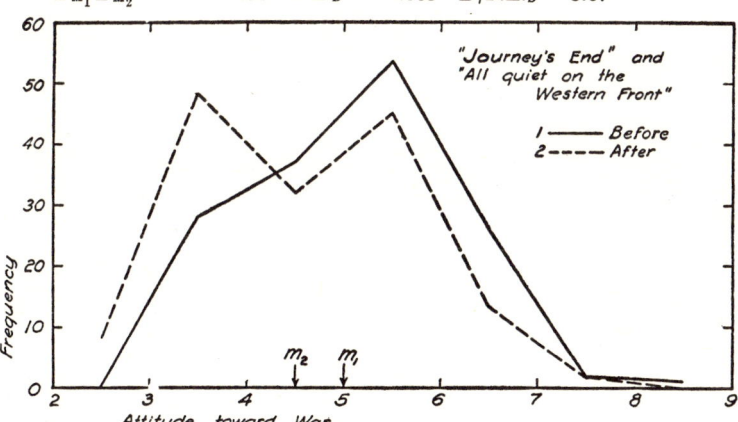

Unfavorable   FIGURE 20   Favorable

MOOSEHEART, ILLINOIS

148 Children of Grades 6–12 Inclusive

Mean$_1$ (before) = 5.06   P.E.M.$_1$ = .058 σ_1 = 1.04 r_{12} = .37
Mean$_2$ (after) = 4.52   P.E.M.$_2$ = .061 σ_2 = 1.10
$D_{M_1 - M_2}$ = .54   P.E.$_D$ = .067   D/P.E.$_D$ = 8.06

combined group before the pictures were shown was 4.99; after, 4.53, a change of .46 of a scale step with a P.E.$_D$ of .0323 and a ratio of the difference to the P.E.$_D$ of 14.24.

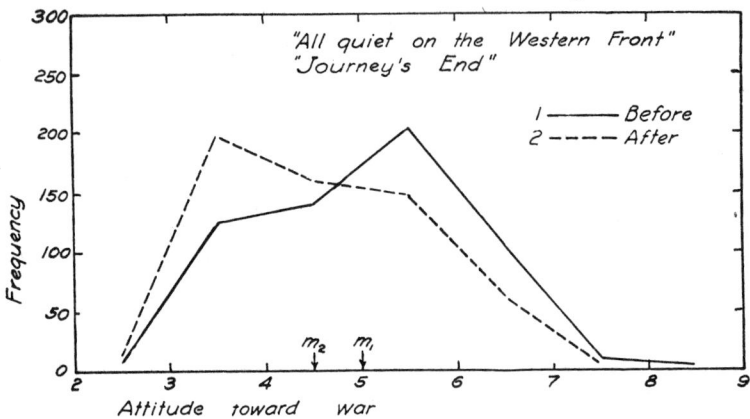

FIGURE 21
MOOSEHEART, ILLINOIS
595 Children of Grades 6-12 Inclusive

Mean$_1$ (before) = 4.99   P.E.M.$_1$ = .029 σ_1 = 1.06 r_{12} = .38
Mean$_2$ (after) = 4.53   P.E.M.$_2$ = .029 σ_2 = 1.06
D$_{M_1 - M_2}$ = .46   P.E.$_D$ = .0323   D/P.E.$_D$ = 14.24

Three crime pictures and the punishment of criminals

The second series of experiments utilized a similar grouping and studied the effect of three films on attitude toward punishment of criminals. The attitude scale used in this experiment was the same as the one used at Watseka, Illinois (see page 28).

The set-up of this series was as follows:

July 27, 1931—Grades six to twelve inclusive took the scale of attitude toward the punishment of criminals.
August 5, 1931—Groups A, B, and C saw "Big House."
August 6, 1931—Group C took the attitude scale.

August 12, 1931—Groups A, B, and D saw "Numbered Men."
August 13, 1931—Groups B and D took the attitude scale.
August 19, 1931—Groups A, C, and D saw "The Criminal Code."
August 20, 1931—Groups A, C, D, and E took the attitude scale.

The above arrangement gave the following data:
(1) Group A—Cumulative effect of the three films "Big House," "Numbered Men," and "The Criminal Code."
(2) Group B—Cumulative effect of the two films, "Big House" and "Numbered Men."
(3) Group C—Single effect of "Big House."
Cumulative effect of "Big House" and "The Criminal Code."
(4) Group D—Single effect of "Numbered Men."
Cumulative effect of "Numbered Men" and "The Criminal Code."
(5) Group E—Attitude scores at three weeks' interval with no interposed propaganda.

A summary of the results is given in the following table:

Film	N	M_1	M_2	D	P.E.$_D$	D/P.E.$_D$
"Big House"	138	5.14	5.13	−.01	.079	x
"Numbered Men"	168	5.23	5.27	+.04	.065	x
"Big House" and "Numbered Men"	143	5.23	5.03	−.20	.066	3.0
"Big House" and "The Criminal Code"	138	5.14	4.97	−.17	.076	2.2
"Numbered Men" and "The Criminal Code"	168	5.23	4.95	−.28	.072	3.9
"Big House," "Numbered Men," "The Criminal Code"	139	5.22	4.83	−.39	.059	6.7
No film	167	4.95	4.98	+.03	.067	x

The above table shows that neither "Big House" nor "Numbered Men" had a measurable effect on the children's attitudes; however, the group who saw both pictures showed a significant change in attitude toward the punishment of criminals as a result of seeing the films. The effect of the films "The Criminal Code" and "Big House" was smaller than the effect of "The Criminal Code" combined with "Numbered Men." This difference may be partially explained by the fact that the former group had a lower score before. The group who saw all three pictures showed the greatest change in attitude. The results of this experiment indicate that the effect of motion pictures on attitude is cumulative. A combination of two pictures on the same issue, neither of which has a measurable effect, may show a significant change of attitude toward the issue in question. The cumulative effect of motion pictures is illustrated further by the effect of a combination of three films on the same issue.

The results for each group are presented graphically below.

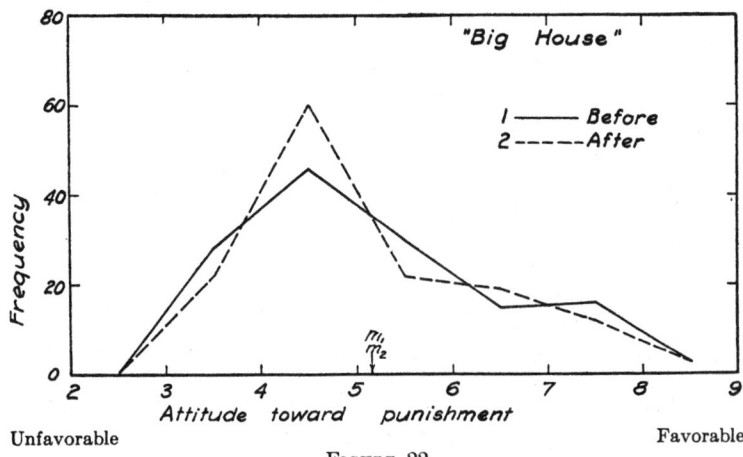

FIGURE 22

MOOSEHEART, ILLINOIS

138 Children of Grades 6-12 Inclusive

$Mean_1$ (before) = 5.14 $P.E.M._1$ = .078 σ_1 = 1.35 r_{12} = .46
$Mean_2$ (after) = 5.13 $P.E.M._2$ = .075 σ_2 = 1.30
$D_{M_1 - M_2}$ = .01 $P.E._D$ = .079 $D/P.E._D = x$

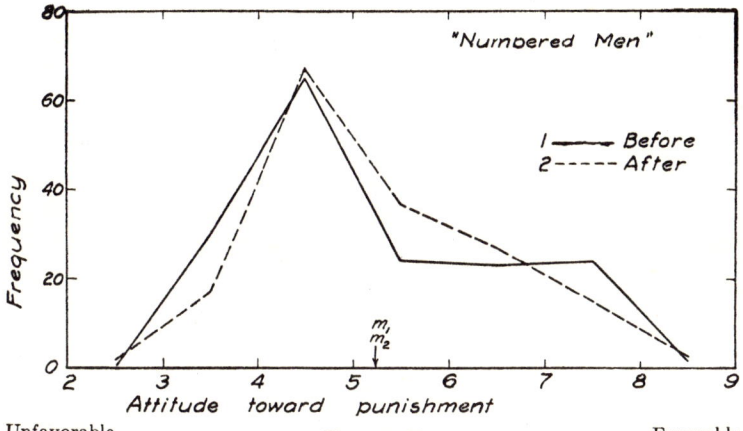

Unfavorable   FIGURE 23   Favorable

MOOSEHEART, ILLINOIS

168 Children of Grades 6-12 Inclusive

Mean_1 (before) = 5.23 $\text{P.E.M.}_1 = .072$ $\sigma_1 = 1.38$ $r_{12} = .55$
Mean_2 (after) = 5.27 $\text{P.E.M.}_2 = .064$ $\sigma_2 = 1.22$
$D_{M_1 - M_2}$ = .04 P.E._D = .065 $D/\text{P.E.}_D = x$

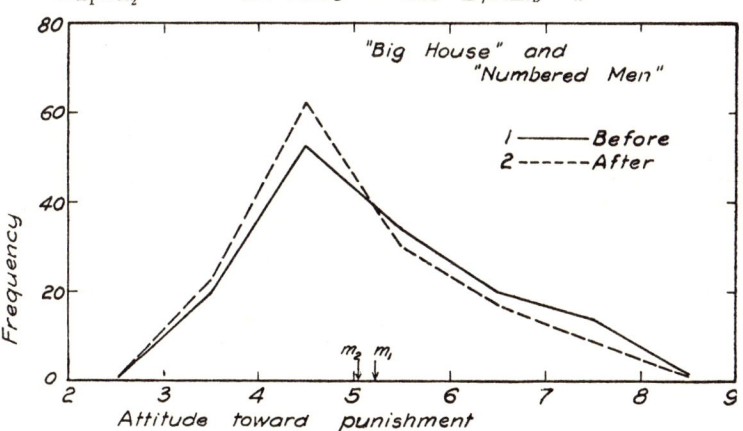

Unfavorable   FIGURE 24   Favorable

MOOSEHEART, ILLINOIS

143 Children of Grades 6-12 Inclusive

Mean_1 (before) = 5.23 $\text{P.E.M.}_1 = .068$ $\sigma_1 = 1.21$ $r_{12} = .50$
Mean_2 (after) = 5.03 $\text{P.E.M.}_2 = .064$ $\sigma_2 = 1.14$
$D_{M_1 - M_2}$ = .20 P.E._D = .0664 $D/\text{P.E.}_D = 3.0$

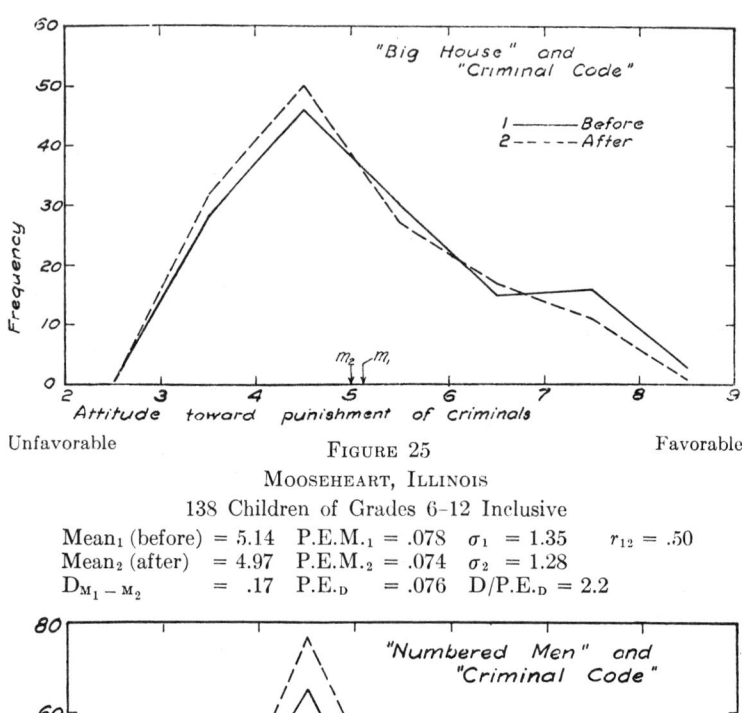

Unfavorable   FIGURE 25   Favorable
MOOSEHEART, ILLINOIS
138 Children of Grades 6-12 Inclusive

Mean_1 (before) = 5.14 $\text{P.E.M.}_1 = .078$ $\sigma_1 = 1.35$ $r_{12} = .50$
Mean_2 (after) = 4.97 $\text{P.E.M.}_2 = .074$ $\sigma_2 = 1.28$
$D_{M_1 - M_2}$ = .17 $\text{P.E.}_D = .076$ $D/\text{P.E.}_D = 2.2$

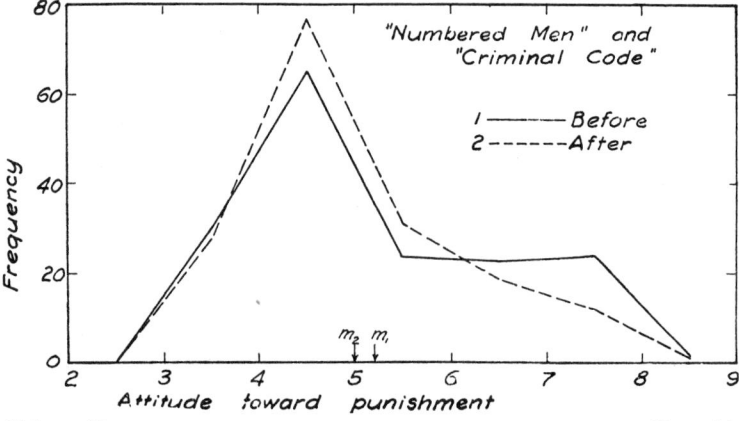

Unfavorable   FIGURE 26   Favorable
MOOSEHEART, ILLINOIS
168 Children of Grades 6-12 Inclusive

Mean_1 (before) = 5.23 $\text{P.E.M.}_1 = .072$ $\sigma_1 = 1.38$ $r_{12} = .42$
Mean_2 (after) = 4.95 $\text{P.E.M.}_2 = .061$ $\sigma_2 = 1.18$
$D_{M_1 - M_2}$ = .28 $\text{P.E.}_D = .072$ $D/\text{P.E.}_D = 3.9$

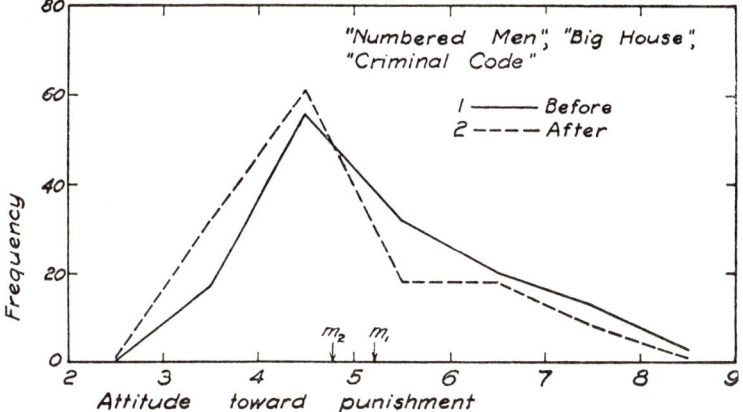

FIGURE 27
MOOSEHEART, ILLINOIS
139 Children of Grades 6–12 Inclusive

Mean_1 (before) = 5.22 $P.E.M._1 = .070$ $\sigma_1 = 1.23$ $r_{12} = .65$
Mean_2 (after) = 4.83 $P.E.M._2 = .070$ $\sigma_2 = 1.22$
$D_{M_1 - M_2}$ = .39 $P.E._D = .059$ $D/P.E._D = 6.7$

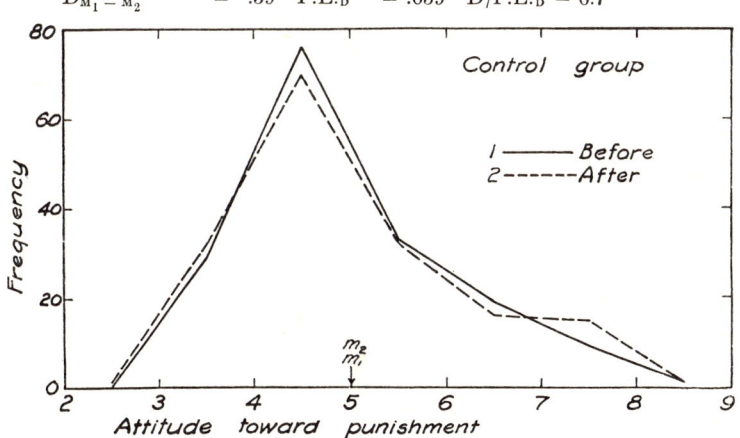

FIGURE 28
MOOSEHEART, ILLINOIS
167 Children of Grades 6–12 Inclusive

Mean_1 (before) = 4.95 $P.E.M._1 = .058$ $\sigma_1 = 1.12$ $r_{12} = .41$
Mean_2 (after) = 4.98 $P.E.M._2 = .064$ $\sigma_2 = 1.22$
$D_{M_1 - M_2}$ = .03 $P.E._D = .067$ $D/P.E._D = x$

Figure 29 shows the distribution of attitude toward the punishment of criminals for the entire experimental group, exclusive of the control group. The mean attitude of the 588 children in the total group (excluding Group E) was 5.21 before the pictures were shown and 4.95 after. The difference is .26 with a P.E.$_D$ of .0332, giving a ratio of 7.83.

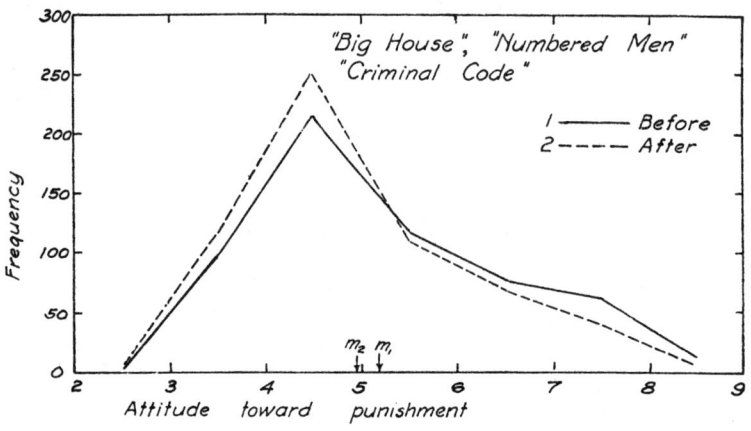

FIGURE 29
MOOSEHEART, ILLINOIS
588 Children of Grades 6–12 Inclusive

Mean$_1$ (before) = 5.21 P.E.M.$_1$ = .036 σ_1 = 1.30 r_{12} = .54
Mean$_2$ (after) = 4.95 P.E.M.$_2$ = .033 σ_2 = 1.20
$D_{M_1 - M_2}$ = .26 P.E.$_D$ = .0332 D/P.E.$_D$ = 7.83

CHAPTER IV

THE PERSISTENCE OF EFFECT

THE experiments reported have been concerned with the measurement of the effect of motion pictures on social attitudes. The effect of a motion picture was measured by means of an attitude scale given a week or two before and the day after the film was shown. These measurements of the immediate effect of a film showed, in a number of experiments, very striking changes in attitude. We were also interested in studying the persistence of the effect by repeated measurement of the attitudes of the children who had participated in the experiments. We present below the results of six studies of the persistence of the effect of a motion picture.

Attitudes toward Germans

In Genoa, Illinois, the experiment conducted showed a change of attitude favorable to the Germans, as the result of seeing the film "Four Sons." As previously reported, the effect of the motion picture was measured the day after the children saw the film. After an interval of six months the scale of attitude toward the Germans was given again. The group included 87 of the students who had seen the picture. The mean attitude of this group on April 17, 1930, was 5.66; the day after the picture was shown (April 29, 1930) it was 5.19; about six months later (October 9, 1930) the mean attitude of the group was 5.10. In other words, the children were still more favorable to the Germans six months later than they were the day after they saw the film "Four Sons." We suggest as an explanation the fact that there was no theater in Genoa regularly showing pictures and that the motion picture "Four Sons" was probably the subject of considerable comment and discussion among the children because a motion picture was a relatively rare occurrence for this group. Figure 30 gives the three frequency distributions. The statistical facts for each distribution are given below the figure.

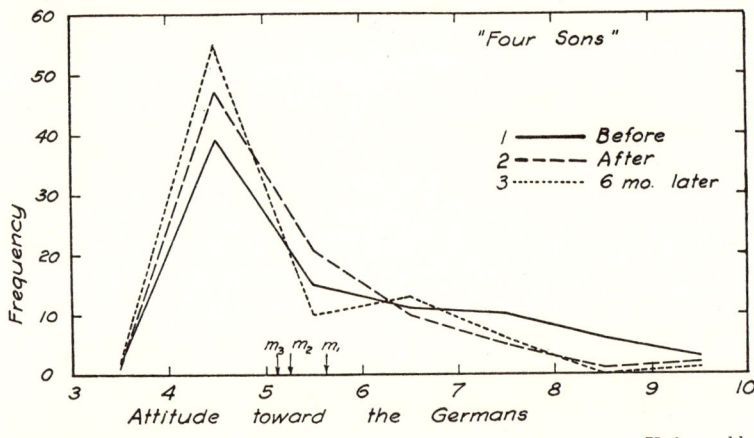

FIGURE 30
GENOA TOWNSHIP HIGH SCHOOL, GENOA, ILLINOIS
87 Children of Grades 7-11 Inclusive

Mean_1 (before) $= 5.74$
Mean_2 (after) $= 5.27 \quad D_{1-2} = .47 \quad \sigma_1 = 1.52 \quad r_{13} = .57$
Mean_3 (6 mos. later) $= 5.16 \quad D_{1-3} = .58 \quad \sigma_3 = 1.03$
$\dfrac{D_{1-3}}{D_{1-2}} = \dfrac{.58}{.47} = 1.23 \qquad \text{P.E.}_{D_{1-3}} = .0911 \qquad \dfrac{D_{1-3}}{\text{P.E.}_{D_{1-3}}} = 6.37$

The paired comparison schedule of nationalities was also repeated, and the results showed the Germans in the same relative position (see Figure 2) six months later that they were in the day after the children saw the motion picture "Four Sons."

Attitude toward Chinese

In Geneva where the motion picture "Son of the Gods" was shown and its effects on the high school students' attitudes toward the Chinese measured, the scale of attitude toward the Chinese was given after an interval of five months, and a fourth time after an interval of nineteen months. The means of the group before and after were recalculated including only the students (117) who took the scale the third time. Consequently these means vary slightly from those reported for the original group.

Figure 31 shows the frequency distributions for the group the week before, the day after seeing the film "Son of the Gods," and five months later. The three means are as follows: before, 6.57, day after, 5.26, five months later, 5.76. The third measurement shows that the attitudes of the children toward the Chinese had returned part way toward the position before the picture was seen, but the children were still decidedly more favorable toward the Chinese than they had been five months previously, before the film was shown. The statistical facts about the three distributions are given on page 54 the figure.

The difference five months later (.81) divided by the difference measured the day following the presentation of the motion picture (1.31) gives a ratio of .62. We may say that the effect of the film was still definitely present after the interval of five months.

The scale of attitude toward the Chinese was given in the Geneva High School again in the fall of 1931, nineteen months after the original experiment was conducted. The group was much smaller, because two classes had graduated,

54   MOTION PICTURES AND ATTITUDES OF CHILDREN

but a comparison of the four means for the 76 students who had participated in the original experiment and who were still available shows that the children's attitudes, after an

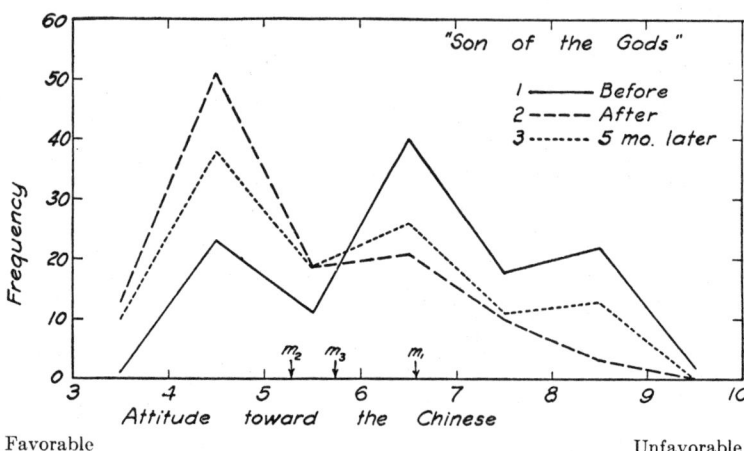

FIGURE 31
GENEVA HIGH SCHOOL, GENEVA, ILLINOIS
117 Children of Grades 9-11 Inclusive

Mean_1 (before) = 6.57
Mean_2 (after) = 5.26 $D_{1-2} = 1.31$ $\sigma_1 = 1.45$ $r_{13} = .59$
Mean_3 (5 mos. later) = 5.76 $D_{1-3} = .81$ $\sigma_3 = 1.48$

$\dfrac{D_{1-3}}{D_{1-2}} = \dfrac{.81}{1.31} = .62$ $\text{P.E.}_{D_{1-3}} = .0827$ $\dfrac{D_{1-3}}{\text{P.E.}_{D_{1-3}}} = 9.79$

interval of over a year and a half, still showed the effect of the film "Son of the Gods." The means were as follows:

M_1—May 17, 1930 is 6.61 $N = 76$ (Before seeing the film)
M_2—May 27, 1930 is 5.19 $N = 76$ (The day after seeing the film)
M_3—Oct. 28, 1930 is 5.72 $N = 71$ (5 months after seeing the film)
M_4—Dec. 2, 1931 is 5.76 $N = 76$ (19 months after seeing the film)

$M_1 - M_2 = 1.42$ $\dfrac{M_1 - M_3}{M_1 - M_2} = \dfrac{.89}{1.42} = .63$
$M_1 - M_3 = .89$
$M_1 - M_4 = .85$ $\dfrac{M_1 - M_4}{M_1 - M_2} = \dfrac{.85}{1.42} = .60$

The data indicate that the effect of the film "Son of the Gods" is present after an interval of nineteen months. The children's attitudes are still, after that interval, definitely more favorable to the Chinese than previous to the viewing of the film. The change in attitude from October, 1930, to December, 1931, shows very little return toward the original position as measured on May 17, 1930. The effect of the picture on attitude, as measured the day after the picture was seen, has been partially lost after an interval of five months. The loss during the succeeding fourteen months, is, however, very small, as indicated by the ratios given above.

It may be noted that the difference $M_1 - M_2$ is larger for this group of 76 than for the group of 117 who participated in the first measurement of persistence. The ratio of $M_1 - M_3$ to $M_1 - M_2$ is comparable for the two groups, however, indicating that the percentage of the original effect which was still present was practically the same, although the absolute change varied for the two groups.

Attitude toward gambling

The paired comparison of minor crimes was given a third time at Mendota, Illinois, to study the persistence of the effect of "Street of Chance" on the children's attitudes toward gambling.

The schedule was given on May 15, 1930, the motion picture was shown on May 22, the scale was given the second time on May 23, and five months later on October 15, 1930.

Figure 32 shows the scale values for each crime before, after, and five months later. The scale value for gambler, which changed markedly after the children had seen the film, returned part way toward its first position, but the effect of the film is still evident.

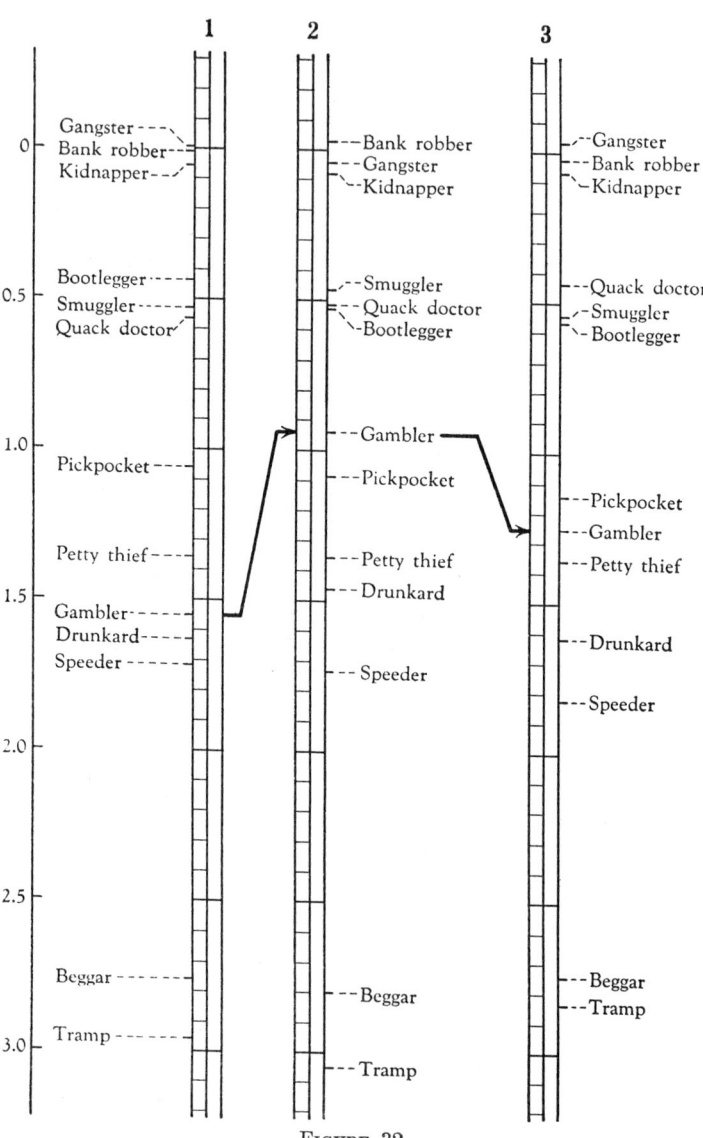

FIGURE 32
SERIOUSNESS OF CRIMES AS JUDGED BY 240 SCHOOL CHILDREN IN MENDOTA, ILLINOIS, BEFORE, AFTER, AND FIVE MONTHS AFTER SEEING THE FILM "STREET OF CHANCE"

Attitude toward punishment of criminals

In Watseka, Illinois, the scale of attitude toward punishment of criminals, which had been used to measure the effect of the picture "The Criminal Code," was given twice more after intervals of two and one-half months and nine months, respectively.

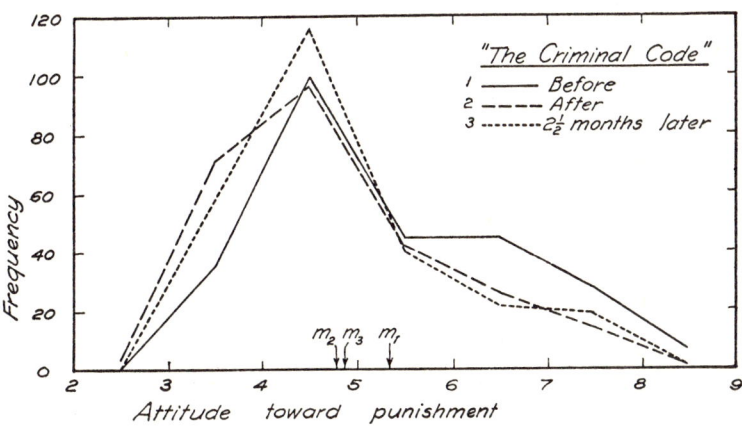

Unfavorable   Favorable

FIGURE 33

WATSEKA COMMUNITY HIGH SCHOOL, WATSEKA, ILLINOIS
257 Children of Grades 7-12 Inclusive

Mean_1 (before) = 5.33
Mean_2 (after) = 4.78 $D_{1-2} = .55$ $\sigma_1 = 1.33$ $r_{13} = .54$
Mean_3 (2½ mos. later) = 4.85 $D_{1-3} = .48$ $\sigma_3 = 1.19$

$$\frac{D_{1-3}}{D_{1-2}} = \frac{.48}{.55} = .87 \qquad \text{P.E.}_{D_{1-3}} = .0511 \qquad \frac{D_{1-3}}{\text{P.E.}_{D_{1-3}}} = 9.39$$

In Figure 33 the frequency distributions before and after and two and one-half months later are given. The means for the three distributions are 5.33, 4.78, and 4.85 respectively. The effect of the motion picture on the children's attitudes toward the punishment of criminals is still very evident after the interval of two and one-half months.

The scale was given the fourth time in December, 1931. One hundred ninety-five children who had participated in the experiment took the scale. The means for this group in each of the four applications appear below.

M_1 February 19, 1931 5.42
M_2 March   5, 1931 4.84
M_3 May   25, 1931 4.91
M_4 December   2, 1931 4.97

$M_1 - M_2 = .58$ $\dfrac{M_1 - M_3}{M_1 - M_2} = .88$
$M_1 - M_3 = .51$
$M_1 - M_4 = .45$ $\dfrac{M_1 - M_4}{M_1 - M_2} = .78$

It is obvious that the effect of the motion picture was present nine months after the children saw the film. Eighty-eight per cent of the effect measured the day after the picture was still present after ten weeks; after nine months 78% of the effect remained. We conclude that the effect of this motion picture on attitude persists for a considerable period of time, and although the effect is smaller after an interval it is still very evident.

Attitude toward war

In Paxton, Illinois, we found that the film "All Quiet on the Western Front" made the children less favorable to war. The experiment was conducted in March, 1931. In November, 1931, nine months later, the scale of attitude toward war was given again.

The change in attitude as a result of the picture was .60 of a scale step, a change in the direction of pacificism. The ratio of the difference to the $P.E._D$ was 13.2 which was undoubtedly a significant change. The mean attitude of the group eight months later was 4.64, a change in the opposite direction. The difference between M_1 and M_3 was .30 scale step in the direction favorable to war. The change of attitude represented by the difference between M_2 and M_3 was .90 scale step in the direction favorable to war. The three frequency distributions for the group of 138 students are given in Figure 34.

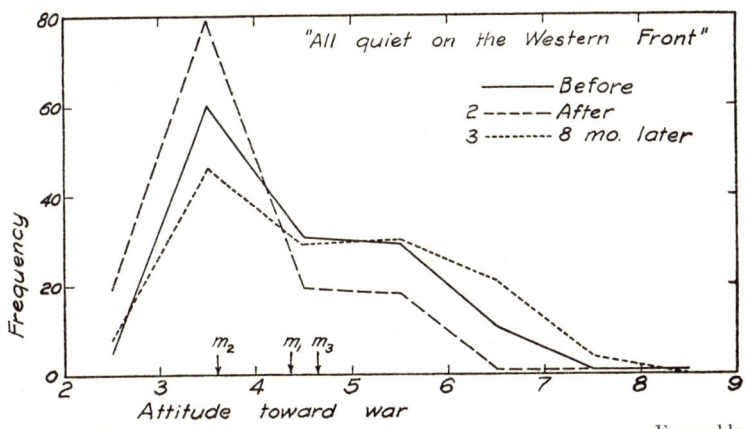

Unfavorable   Favorable

FIGURE 34

PAXTON COMMUNITY HIGH SCHOOL, PAXTON, ILLINOIS
138 Children of Grades 9–12 Inclusive

Mean₁ (before) = 4.34
Mean₂ (after) = 3.74 D_{1-2} = .60 σ_1 = 1.12 r_{13} = .53
Mean₃ (8 mos. later) = 4.64 D_{1-3} = +.30 σ_3 = 1.26

$$P.E._{D_{1-3}} = .0665 \quad \frac{D_{1-3}}{P.E._{D_{1-3}}} = 4.51$$

We have no explanation for this effect. There was, undoubtedly, some interposed propaganda which made the children more favorable toward war. We are trying to discover whether anything happened in the community during the interval between March and November, 1931, which might explain the fact that the children's attitudes were more favorable to war at the third measurement in November than they were in March, in spite of the fact that the interposed film had a significant effect on their attitudes in the opposite direction. The change is obviously too large to be attributed to chance error in measurement.

Attitude toward the Negro

In the study reported earlier in this paper we found that the picture "The Birth of a Nation" had a striking effect on the attitudes of a group of children toward the Negro. The scale of attitude toward the Negro which had been given on May 18, 1931 (before the picture), and May 27, 1931 (the day after the picture), was given again on October 20, 1931.

Figure 35 gives the three frequency distributions. The statistical facts for the three distributions are given below.

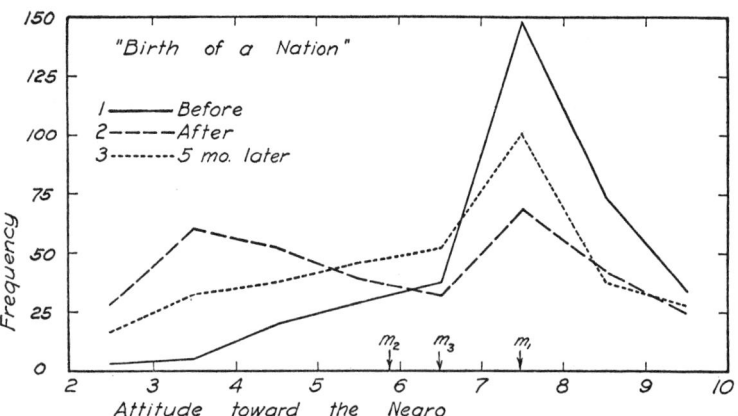

FIGURE 35
CRYSTAL LAKE HIGH SCHOOL, CRYSTAL LAKE, ILLINOIS
434 Children of Grades 6–11 Inclusive

$Mean_1$ (before) = 7.46
$Mean_2$ (after) = 5.93 $D_{1-2} = 1.53$ $\sigma_1 = 1.40$ $r_{13} = .51$
$Mean_3$ (5 mos. later) = 6.51 $D_{1-3} = .95$ $\sigma_3 = 1.90$

$$\frac{D_{1-3}}{D_{1-2}} = \frac{.95}{1.53}$$

$P.E._{D_{1-3}} = .0609$ $\dfrac{D_{1-3}}{P.E._{D_{1-3}}} = 15.59$

If the three means are compared, it may be noted that the mean attitude of the group five months after the picture was shown was much less favorable to the Negro than before the picture was seen. Although the attitudes of the group had returned part way toward the position represented by the first distribution of attitude, the effect of the picture "The Birth of a Nation" on the children's attitudes toward the Negro was still definitely present eight months after the film was shown.

Mooseheart experiments

The attitude scales were given at Mooseheart two months and four months after the pictures were shown to study the persistence of the effect found in the original experiment. The findings are presented below.

SCALE OF ATTITUDE TOWARD WAR

	M	N	D		
M_1 Mean attitude of group before seeing the pictures	4.99	595			
M_2 After seeing pictures	4.53	595	M_1	M_2 =	.46
M_3 Two months later	4.75	572	M_1	M_3 =	.24
M_4 Four months later	4.89	571	M_1	M_4 =	.10

We conclude that the effect of the pictures "All Quiet on the Western Front" and "Journey's End" on the children's attitudes toward war was still evident after an interval of two months, but present only in a slight degree after an interval of four months.

The change in attitude toward punishment of criminals as a result of seeing the pictures "Big House," "Numbered Men," and "The Criminal Code" was not as marked as the effect of the pictures "All Quiet on the Western Front" and "Journey's End" on attitude toward war, but the persistence of the effect was greater. The following table presents the findings.

SCALE OF ATTITUDE TOWARD PUNISHMENT OF CRIMINALS

	M	N	D	
M_1 Mean attitude of group before seeing the pictures	5.21	588		
M_2 After seeing pictures	4.95	588	M_1	$M_2 = .26$
M_3 Two months later	4.95	559	M_1	$M_3 = .26$
M_4 Four months later	4.92	549	M_1	$M_4 = .29$

The children were more lenient in their attitude toward punishment of criminals after seeing the films "Big House," "Numbered Men," and "The Criminal Code" ($D_{M_1} - _{M_2} = 7.83 \times P.E._D$), and the effect of the pictures was undiminished after an interval of four months.

We conclude that the effect of motion pictures on children's attitudes, measured by means of attitude scales given a week or two weeks before and the day following the presentation of the film, persists for a considerable period of time. The measurements of persistence which have been presented indicate in each case, with the exception of Paxton, that the change in attitude occasioned by a motion picture is lasting. The table on page 63 summarizes the amount of the effect measured which is present after various intervals.

This summary is presented without regard to the amount of change as a result of the picture but is given to show that the effects found are very definitely lasting. The longest interval between an original measurement of attitude and a measurement of the persistence of a change in attitude as a result of seeing a motion picture is nineteen months; the data presented indicate, however, that the effect of a

The Persistence of Effect

motion picture on social attitudes probably persists for a much longer time.

Place	Film	No. in Exp. Group	Interval	Per Cent of Effect Remaining
Watseka, Illinois	"The Criminal Code"	257	2½ months	87%
Watseka, Illinois	"The Criminal Code"	195	9 months	78%
Geneva, Illinois	"Son of the Gods"	117	5 months	62%
Geneva, Illinois	"Son of the Gods"	76	19 months	60%
Crystal Lake, Illinois	"The Birth of a Nation"	350	5 months	62%
Genoa, Illinois	"Four Sons"	87	6 months	123%
Paxton, Illinois	"All Quiet on the Western Front"	138	8 months	A change in the opposite direction.
Mooseheart, Illinois	"All Quiet on the Western Front" and "Journey's End"	572	2 months	52%
Mooseheart, Illinois	"All Quiet on the Western Front" and "Journey's End"	571	4 months	22%
Mooseheart, Illinois	"The Big House," "Numbered Men," and "The Criminal Code"	559	2 months	100%
Mooseheart, Illinois	"The Big House," "Numbered Men," and "The Criminal Code"	549	4 months	111%

CHAPTER V
CONCLUSIONS

IN the studies reported in this paper, measurement of the effect of motion pictures on social attitudes has been demonstrated. The general plan of the experiments was to measure the attitudes of a group of children by means of an attitude scale or a paired comparison schedule, to show the children a motion picture which had been judged as having affective value on the issue in question, and to measure the attitudes of the children again after the picture had been shown. The interval between the first application of the scale and the motion picture varied from one to three weeks; the second application of the scale took place the day after the children saw the film.

There were two restrictions on the number of issues which were studied in the experiments. Obviously, the issues were restricted to those for which we could find suitable films. The second restriction concerned the subjects who participated in our experiments. It is highly probable that motion pictures could be found which might affect attitude toward sex, marriage, divorce, birth control, or illegitimacy, for example, but it was not deemed advisable to use such films with groups of children of the seventh through the twelfth grades.

The issues which were studied include attitude toward nationality and race, crime, the punishment of criminals, capital punishment, and prohibition. The most striking change in attitude found in our experiments was the change in attitude toward the Negro as a result of seeing the picture "The Birth of a Nation." The film "Son of the Gods" showed a definite change in attitude favorable to the Chinese, and "Four Sons" made the children more favorable toward the Germans. "The Criminal Code" made a group more lenient in their attitude toward punishment of criminals. The pictures "Big House" and "Numbered Men" in combination had a similar effect.

A group of high school children were less favorable toward war after seeing "All Quiet on the Western Front." One group who saw "Journey's End" showed no change in attitude toward war, a second group showed a small change in the direction of pacifism. A group of high school children were more severe in their judgment of gambling after seeing the picture "Street of Chance." The motion pictures used to study change in attitude toward capital punishment and prohibition showed no effect on the children's attitudes.

Some of the experiments suggested that the effect of the motion pictures was greater on the younger children. The evidence on this question is not conclusive. The experiment which included the widest range and which was planned especially to study this point did not give positive results.

The problem of the cumulative effect of two or more pictures pertaining to the same issue was studied in the experiments at Mooseheart. The results indicate that two pictures, neither of which has a significant effect on attitude, may have such an effect on the attitudes of a group who see both pictures. It was found that three pictures, seen at the intervals of a week, had a cumulative effect on attitude.

A question arose concerning the persistence of the effect of a motion picture on attitude. The changes in attitude, as a result of seeing a picture, were measured the day following the presentation of the film. The attitudes of the students who had participated in the experiments were measured again after intervals ranging from ten weeks to nineteen months. These subsequent measures of attitudes showed that the effect of a motion picture on attitude persists, although there is some return toward the position held before the picture was presented.

In conclusion we may say that the experiments we conducted show that motion pictures have definite, lasting effects on the social attitudes of children and that a number of pictures pertaining to the same issue may have a cumulative effect on attitude.

APPENDIX

ONE of the projects undertaken was the construction of a scale of attitude toward the "movies." We wish to present this scale and to describe the method of its construction.[5]

The original collection of opinions about the movies consisted of 258 statements. These opinions, each of which reflects an attitude toward the movies, vary from statements decidedly in favor of the movies through neutral statements to those very much opposed to the movies. They were obtained from literature on the subject, from conversation, and from direct questioning of subjects whose education and experience varied from that of seventh grade children to that of graduate students in the university.[6]

Each statement was then typewritten on a separate card. As a preliminary method of eliminating the most unsatisfactory and retaining the best statements, as well as to get an approximate idea of the scale values of the statements, the method of equal-appearing intervals [7] was used with a small group of sorters. Twenty-five people, who had some understanding of the method being used and who were carefully chosen to make sure that the directions would be thoroughly understood and complied with, sorted the cards into eleven piles according to the following instructions:

"These cards contain statements about the value of the movies. Please arrange these cards in eleven piles so that those expressing

[5] Thurstone, L. L., "A Scale for Measuring Attitude toward the Movies," *Journal of Educational Research*, September, 1930, pp. 89–94.
[6] Acknowledgment is made to Miss Marie Thiele for the collection of the original set of statements.
[7] Thurstone, L. L., "Attitudes Can Be Measured," *American Journal of Sociology*, XXXIII, January, 1928, pp. 529–554.

attitudes most strongly in favor of the movies are in pile one, those which are neutral are in pile six, and those which are most strongly against the movies are in the eleventh pile. The intermediate piles should represent steps in appreciation or depreciation of the movies.

"Do not try to get the same number of cards in each pile. They are not evenly distributed.

"The numbers on the cards are code numbers and have nothing to do with the arrangement in piles.

"You will find it easier to sort them if you look over a number of the slips, chosen at random, before you begin to sort."

The results of these twenty-five sortings were tabulated to show in which piles each statement was placed by the group of sorters. The scale values were then determined graphically. As an example of the method used one of the graphs is reproduced on page 69.

The figure represents statement Number 101 of the original group, which happens to be retained in the final scale as Number 12. The graph shows that all the sorters classified the statement as favorable to the movies. The statement reads "Movies increase one's appreciation of beauty." The curve crosses the 50% level at the value of 2.9. This scale value is such that half the readers classified it as favorable to movies and half of them as less favorable.

The scale value is indicated by the arrowhead on the base line. The lighter lines on either side of the arrowhead indicate the quartile range of values assigned to the statements. The Q-value in this case is 1.10. This is a measure of the ambiguity of the statement.

For the application of a more exact scaling technique 100 statements were chosen from the 258. The choice was based on the following criteria:

(1) A continuity of scale values, *i.e.*, a selection of approximately the same number from each region of the scale.

Appendix

(2) Selection of statements with small Q-values.
(3) Diction and clearness of the statement itself.

The average Q-value of the statements retained was 1.18 with a range of .40 to 1.90; while the average Q-value of those statements not retained was 1.44 with a range of .50 to 3.25.

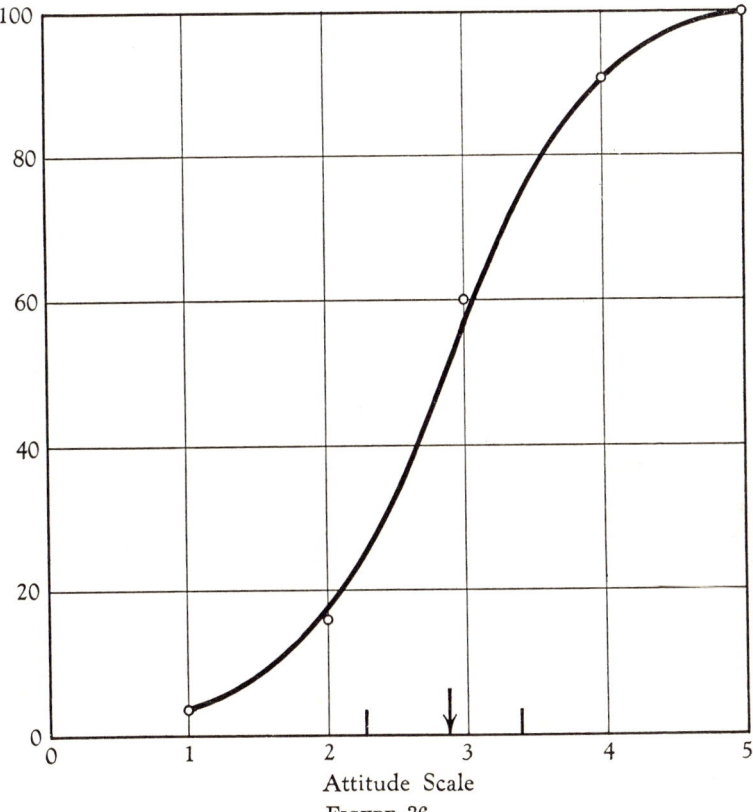

FIGURE 36

STATEMENT NUMBER 101, "MOVIES INCREASE ONE'S APPRECIATION OF BEAUTY"

$Q_1 = 2.25$ $Q_3 = 3.45$
$M = 2.90$ $Q = 1.10$

Two hundred sets of these 100 statements were then printed on three by five cards.

The 100 statements were then arranged in ten envelopes for rank order sortings. The first envelope contained the fifteen statements most strongly in favor of the movies as determined by the preliminary scaling method. The second envelope contained statements 8 to 22, the third envelope 18 to 32, and so on, the tenth envelope containing statements 86 to 100. Thus it is seen that fifty of the 100 statements were repeated in two envelopes.

The statements in each envelope were in random order and the envelopes were also put in random order. The ten envelopes of statements were presented to the people who were to sort them with the following directions:

"Each envelope in this series contains fifteen cards. On each card is a statement about the movies. Some of these statements are in favor of the movies, and some of them are against the movies. Will you arrange the fifteen statements in each envelope so that the statement which is most in favor of the movies is on top, face up, and the statement which is least in favor of the movies or most strongly against the movies is on the bottom? The cards should all be arranged so that each card is more in favor of the movies than the card under it and less in favor of the movies than the card above it.

"In considering each statement ask yourself this question:

"'How strongly in favor of the movies is a person who endorses or agrees with this statement?' Try to disregard your own attitude toward the statements.

"The identification numbers on the cards have no significance."

Two hundred people sorted the statements by the above directions, putting the fifteen statements in each envelope in rank order.

The results of these sortings were tabulated, and from the tabulations we determined the proportion of times each

Appendix

statement was rated as more strongly in favor of the movies than every other statement. From these proportions the scale separations of the statements in each envelope were determined from the formula: [8]

$$b-a = \frac{\Sigma X_{ka} - \Sigma X_{kb}}{n}$$

in which $(b-a)$ is the scale separation between a and b.

X_{ka} is the deviation $(k-a)$ in terms of the standard deviation. It is ascertained from the probability tables by means of the observed proportions $k > a$.

X_{kb} is the deviation $(k - b)$ in terms of the standard deviation.

n is the number of statements minus one.

Since there were overlapping statements in each adjacent pair of envelopes, the scale separations for the whole set of 100 statements could be calculated. The final scale values of the 100 statements ranged from 4.74, the most strongly in favor of the movies, to 0.00, the most strongly against the movies.

The 100 statements were then divided into ten groups, with a range of .5 scale step in each group. Subsequently four statements were selected from each group, arriving at a final attitude scale consisting of forty statements approximately evenly spaced on the scale. The complete scale is given below, and the scale value of each statement is shown in parentheses following its serial number. The statements have been arranged in random order.

[8] Thurstone, L. L., "Method of Paired Comparisons for Social Values" (equation 5, p. 391), *Journal of Abnormal and Social Psychology*, XXI, Jan.—March, 1926, pp. 384–400.

ATTITUDE TOWARD MOVIES

This is a study of attitudes toward the movies. On the following pages you will find a number of statements expressing different attitudes toward the movies.

    ✓ Put a check mark if you agree with the statement.
    ✗ Put a cross if you disagree with the statement.

If you simply cannot decide about a statement you may mark it with a question mark.

This is not an examination. There are no right or wrong answers to these statements. This is simply a study of people's attitudes toward the movies. Please indicate your own attitude by a check mark when you agree and by a cross when you disagree.

1. (1.5) The movies occupy time that should be spent in more wholesome recreation.
2. (1.3) I am tired of the movies; I have seen too many poor ones.
3. (4.5) The movies are the best civilizing device ever developed.
4. (0.2) Movies are the most important cause of crime.
5. (2.7) Movies are all right but a few of them give the rest a bad name.
6. (2.6) I like to see movies once in a while but they do disappoint you sometimes.
7. (2.9) I think the movies are fairly interesting.
8. (2.7) Movies are just a harmless pastime.
9. (1.7) The movies to me are just a way to kill time.
10. (4.0) The influence of the movies is decidedly for good.
11. (3.9) The movies are good, clean entertainment.
12. (3.9) Movies increase one's appreciation of beauty.
13. (1.7) I'd never miss the movies if we didn't have them.
14 (2.4) Sometimes I feel that the movies are desirable and sometimes I doubt it.
15. (0.0) It is a sin to go to the movies.
16. (4.3) There would be very little progress without the movies.
17. (4.3) The movies are the most vital form of art to-day.
18. (3.6) A movie is the best entertainment that can be obtained cheaply.
19. (3.4) A movie once in a while is a good thing for everybody.
20. (3.4) The movies are one of the few things I can enjoy by myself.
21. (1.3) Going to the movies is a foolish way to spend your money.
22. (1.1) Moving pictures bore me.
23. (.06) As they now exist movies are wholly bad for children.
24. (0.6) Such a pernicious influence as the movies is bound to weaken the moral fiber of those who attend.
25. (0.3) As a protest against movies we should pledge ourselves never to attend them.
26. (0.1) The movies are the most important single influence for evil.
27. (4.7) The movies are the most powerful influence for good in American life.
28. (2.3) I would go to the movies more often if I were sure of finding something good.
29. (4.1) If I had my choice of anything I wanted to do, I would go to the movies.
30. (2.2) The pleasure people get from the movies just about balances the harm they do.

APPENDIX

31. (2.0) I don't find much that is educational in the current films.
32. (1.9) The information that you obtain from the movies is of little value.
33. (1.0) Movies are a bad habit.
34. (3.3) I like the movies as they are because I go to be entertained not educated.
35. (3.1) On the whole the movies are pretty decent.
36. (0.8) The movies are undermining respect for authority.
37. (2.7) I like to see other people enjoy the movies whether I enjoy them myself or not.
38. (0.3) The movies are to blame for the prevalence of sex offenses.
39. (4.4) The movie is one of the great educational institutions for common people.
40. (0.8) Young people are learning to smoke, drink, and pet from the movies.

In scoring the attitude scale we cannot say that one score is better or worse than another; we can only say that one person's attitude toward the movies is more or less favorable than another person's. It is purely arbitrary that attitudes unfavorable to the movies have lower scale values than favorable attitudes.

Any individual's attitude is measured by the median scale value of all the statements he checks. The person who has the higher score is more favorably inclined toward the movies than the person with a lower score.

For the purpose of comparing groups, the distributions of attitude in each group can be plotted and it can then be said whether and how much one group is more favorable to the movies than another group.[9]

[9] Persons interested in securing copies of the scale for "Attitude toward the Movies" should address Professor L. L. Thurstone, University of Chicago.

INDEX

Aledo, Illinois, 34

Batavia, Illinois, 24
Bird, V. A., 39
Bootlegging, attitude toward, 15-17
Byerly, C. C., 20

Capital punishment, attitude toward, 21-24
Chinese, attitude toward, 17-21, 53-55, 65
Coultrap, H. M., 18
Crime, attitude toward, 13-15
Crystal Lake, Illinois, 35, 60, 63

Dahl, R. E., 34
Darnall, James D., 21
Dean, H. A., 35

Gambling, attitude toward, 13-15, 55-56
Geneseo, Illinois, 21
Geneva, Illinois, 18, 53, 63
Genoa, Illinois, 51, 63
Germans, attitude toward, 5-10, 51-53

Hobson, Clay S., 5

Knox College, 28

McCarty, L. C., 34
Mendota, Illinois, 13, 55
Meyer, L. A., 39
Mooseheart, Illinois, 39, 50, 61-63, 65
Motion pictures experimented with: *Alibi,* 33-35; *All Quiet on the Western Front,* 26-28, 40-44, 58-61, 63, 65; *Big House,* 44-50, 61, 62, 63, 65; *Birth of a Nation,* 35-38, 60-61, 63, 65; *Criminal Code,* 28, 35, 44-50, 57-58, 61-62, 63, 65; *Four Sons,* 5-13, 51-53, 63, 65; *Hide Out,* 15-17; *Journey's End,* 24, 40-44, 63, 65; *Numbered Men,* 44-50, 61-62, 63, 65; *Son of the Gods,* 17-21, 53-55, 63, 65; *Street of Chance,* 13-15, 55, 65; *The Valiant,* 21-24; *Welcome Danger,* 17-21
Movies, cumulative effect of, 39-50; persistence of effect of, 51-63; scale of attitude toward, 67-73

Nationality, attitude toward, 3-4, 5-10
Negro, attitude toward, 35-38, 60-61, 65

Paxton, Illinois, 26, 58, 63
Powers, E. W., 28
Princeton, Illinois, 15
Prohibition, attitude toward, 15-17
Punishment of criminals, 28, 35, 44-50, 57-58, 61-62

Racial attitudes, 1-2, 17-21, 35-38
Reymert, Martin L., 39
Roselle, Ernest N., 39

Shaffer, O. V., 15
Steele, M. E., 13
Storm, H. C., 24
Swinney, John J., 26

Thiele, Marie, 67

War, attitude toward, 10-13, 24-28, 39-44, 58-59, 61
Watseka, Illinois, 28, 57, 63
West Chicago, Illinois, 20
Wiltbank, Rutledge T., 29

THE SOCIAL CONDUCT AND ATTITUDES OF MOVIE FANS

❖

FRANK K. SHUTTLEWORTH
YALE UNIVERSITY

MARK A. MAY
YALE UNIVERSITY

NEW YORK
THE MACMILLAN COMPANY
1933

THIS SERIES OF TWELVE STUDIES OF THE INFLUENCE OF MOTION PICTURES UPON CHILDREN AND YOUTH HAS BEEN MADE BY THE COMMITTEE ON EDUCATIONAL RESEARCH OF THE PAYNE FUND AT THE REQUEST OF THE NATIONAL COMMITTEE FOR THE STUDY OF SOCIAL VALUES IN MOTION PICTURES, NOW THE MOTION PICTURE RESEARCH COUNCIL, 366 MADISON AVENUE, NEW YORK CITY. THE STUDIES WERE DESIGNED TO SECURE AUTHORITATIVE AND IMPERSONAL DATA WHICH WOULD MAKE POSSIBLE A MORE COMPLETE EVALUATION OF MOTION PICTURES AND THEIR SOCIAL POTENTIALITIES

COPYRIGHT, 1933,

BY THE MACMILLAN COMPANY

All rights reserved—no part of this book may be reproduced in any form without permission in writing from the publisher, except by a reviewer who wishes to quote brief passages in connection with a review written for inclusion in magazine or newspaper.

Set up and printed from type. Published November, 1933.

PRINTED IN THE UNITED STATES OF AMERICA

TABLE OF CONTENTS

CHAPTER	PAGE
I. THE GENERAL PLAN OF THE STUDY	1
II. DIFFERENCES BETWEEN MOVIE AND NON-MOVIE CHILDREN IN THE TYPES OF CONDUCT AND ATTITUDES WHICH WERE MEASURED BY THE CHARACTER EDUCATION INQUIRY	7
III. PROCEDURES AND ADEQUACY OF THE ATTITUDES TESTS	27
IV. RESULTS OF THE ATTITUDES SURVEY	39
V. OTHER DIFFERENCES BETWEEN MOVIE AND NON-MOVIE GROUPS	73
VI. SUMMARY AND INTERPRETATIONS	84

APPENDIX

A. THE VALIDITY OF CHILDREN'S REPORTS OF THEIR MOVIE HABITS	95
B. CATALOGUE OF HYPOTHESES WHICH WERE VERIFIED, NOT VERIFIED, OR REVERSED	99
C. A SURVEY OF CERTAIN LEISURE TIME HABITS	107
D. TABLES SHOWING DIFFERENCES IN THE ATTITUDES OF MOVIE AND NON-MOVIE CHILDREN	129
INDEX	141

LIST OF TABLES

TABLE		PAGE
I.	THE RANGE AND FORMS OF CONDUCT AND ATTITUDES IN WHICH MOVIE AND NON-MOVIE CHILDREN WERE CONTRASTED	5
II.	FREQUENCY OF ATTENDANCE REPORTED BY ALL CHILDREN, AND BY THE SELECTED MOVIE AND NON-MOVIE GROUPS, IN POPULATIONS X, Y, AND Z	8
III.	CRITICAL RATIOS SHOWING THE DIFFERENCE BETWEEN MOVIE AND NON-MOVIE GROUPS (OF ALL POPULATIONS) IN REPUTATION AMONG TEACHERS	12
IV.	DEPORTMENT RECORDS FOR MOVIE AND NON-MOVIE CASES IN ALL POPULATIONS, SCORES EXPRESSED IN SIGMA DEVIATIONS	13
V.	PROBABLE SIGNIFICANT DIFFERENCES BETWEEN MOVIE AND NON-MOVIE CHILDREN	26
VI.	SUMMARY TABLE OF FREQUENCY OF MOTION-PICTURE ATTENDANCE IN SEVERAL COMMUNITIES	30
VII.	FINALLY SELECTED AND EQUATED MOVIE AND NON-MOVIE CASES BY SEX, POPULATION, AND AMOUNT OF ATTENDANCE	31
VIII.	PERCENTAGE OF MOVIE AND NON-MOVIE CHILDREN BY SEX AND POPULATION CHECKING "A COLLEGE PROFESSOR" OR "A POPULAR ACTOR" IN RESPONSE TO THE QUESTION "WHICH WOULD YOU RATHER BE?"	41

THE SOCIAL CONDUCT AND ATTITUDES OF MOVIE FANS

CHAPTER I

THE GENERAL PLAN OF THE STUDY

OUT of 100 children in the junior high schools of large urban centers approximately 64 attend the movies once a week. Twenty-seven go two or more times and 7 go three or more times a week. What are the movies doing to the conduct and attitudes of these children?

In *Motion Pictures and the Social Attitudes of Children* Professor Thurstone and his associates have reported studies designed to answer one aspect of this question. By rather precise experimental methods they have shown that it is possible to change children's attitudes in a given direction by showing them a single motion picture which has been selected for the purpose of producing that effect. Our problem in this section of the reports is to determine the influence, not of a single motion picture, but of the child's total motion-picture experience on a wide variety of conducts and a wide range of attitudes. The two problems need to be sharply distinguished. Professor Thurstone shows, for example, that a certain film, "Son of the Gods," created a more favorable attitude toward the Chinese, while another film, "Welcome Danger," created a more unfavorable attitude toward the Chinese. Our problem is to determine the *net effect* of the *general run* of movies on children's attitudes toward the Chinese as well as the net effect on a variety of conducts and a score of other attitudes. The complaint against the movies is not that specific movies influence specific attitudes sometimes favorably and sometimes unfavorably, but rather that the general run of movies and the total of motion-picture experiences of children are unfavorable.

In order to attack this wider problem and at the same time keep within the limits of our time and funds it was necessary to abandon the experimental method and adopt a survey method. The general plan which we have followed in surveying a wide range of conducts and attitudes consists of determining the differences between children who attend the movies very frequently and children who attend only infrequently. This method, however, leaves us without precise experimental controls so that in the end it is difficult to say definitely what part of the observed differences can be attributed to the influence of the movies. We have tried to overcome this limitation by equating our groups, by collecting supplementary data, and by a careful study of the differences themselves. The final chapter presents a more complete statement of the limitations involved and discusses the various possible interpretations of the results.

How the Groups of Movie and Non-Movie Children Were Selected

Under the general plan outlined above our first problem was the selection of groups of children who attend the movies very frequently and very infrequently. All told we have studied more or less intensively some 1400 children selected from among about 7000 children in grades five to nine. The groups surveyed included grades 5 to 8 in three elementary schools in New Haven, Connecticut, and Walden, New York, and seven junior high schools in New Haven, Bridgeport, and Norwalk, Connecticut, and Dayton, Ohio.

The first step was to determine the motion-picture habits of the children in these school populations. In the elementary schools in connection with other questions the children were asked, "How many times a week do you go to the movies?" The answers to this question were supplemented by time schedules filled out Monday of one week, Tuesday of the next week, and so on for seven weeks. In the junior high schools the question was, "How often have you gone to movies (not counting movies during school hours) in the past year? Check on the dotted line *after* the most correct answer. Never been......; Been only a few times......; Go once a month......; Go twice a month......; Three times a month......; Once a week ......; Twice a week......; Three times a week......; Four times a week......; Five times a week......; Six times a week......." The answers to this question were supplemented by asking, "About how many times have you gone to the movies during the past month?" Data presented in Appendix A indicate that the reliability of such reports is at least .60 and possibly .70. While children's reports are far from perfect, they are entirely adequate for the purpose of selecting only the extreme cases and for the purpose of comparing large numbers of cases.

With these data available the second step was to select the extreme cases for more intensive study. Uniformly we selected from each population only the 10 or 15 per cent of children who reported the most frequent attendance for comparison with the 10 or 15 per cent who reported the least frequent attendance. In the interest of brevity we shall hereafter refer to the most frequent attendants as the "movie" and the least frequent attendants as the "non-movie" groups. Among the groups whose attitudes were studied intensively the movie children report on the average 2.8 movies per week while the non-movie children report on the average attendance only a "few times a year." Uniformly these selections were made in such a way that the movie and non-movie groups were alike as to age, sex, school grade, and socio-economic educational home backgrounds. In addition they were equated for intelligence with the exception of one junior high school, and for the nationality of their parents with the exception of the three elementary groups and one junior high school.

The Attitudes and Forms of Conduct on Which the Movie and Non-Movie Groups Were Compared

The attitudes and forms of conduct which were tested in this study were determined partly by fortune and partly by design. Those determined by fortune were inherited from the Character Education Inquiry which had just closed when this study was started. Those determined by design consist of a series of attitudes, opinions, and beliefs based mainly on a collection of complaints against the movies. We have available, then, two rather distinct blocks of data. The first, inherited from the Character Education Inquiry, and collected for quite another purpose, but which happened to fulfill our needs; the second, collected for the specific purposes of this study, namely, to investigate certain complaints against the movies which charged the movies with having a bad effect on the ideals, attitudes, opinions, and beliefs of children.

The following table will show the range of attitudes and conduct which were covered in this study and will also serve as a guide to the presentation of the results.

TABLE I

THE RANGE AND FORMS OF CONDUCT AND ATTITUDES IN WHICH MOVIE AND NON-MOVIE CHILDREN WERE CONTRASTED

A. *From the Character Education Inquiry We Have the Following:*
  1. Eleven measures of the reputation of school children.
     From the teachers:
        (1) The child's deportment grade
        (2) The child's average scholastic grade
        (3) Teacher rating on certain items of conduct
        (4) Teacher rating on certain character traits
     From the pupils:
        (5) Ratings of each other on the "guess who" test
        (6) A sociability or popularity score awarded by classmates
     From selecting and combining elements from (3), (4), and (5) above:
        (7) The child's reputation for honesty
        (8) The child's reputation for coöperativeness
        (9) The child's reputation for persistence
        (10) The child's reputation for self-control
        (11) A total reputation score combining items (7) to (10)
  2. Thirty-seven objective tests of conduct.
        (1) Five tests or samples of coöperative, unselfish, charitable, and altruistic behavior
        (2) Four tests or samples of self-control
        (3) Five tests or samples of persistence
        (4) Twenty-three tests of honesty
  3. Four tests of moral knowledge, social attitudes, and opinions, including several hundred items covering scores of specific attitudes.
  4. Several tests of social background, social instability, intelligence, and other factors.

B. *Attitudes Tests and Questionnaires Designed Especially for This Study Cover the Following Types:*
  1. Attitudes of children toward the heroes and "boobs" of the movies.
  2. Attitudes of children toward peoples of other lands.
  3. Attitudes of children toward prohibition.

4. Attitudes of children toward criminals.
5. Attitudes of children toward sex.
6. Attitudes of children toward school.
7. Attitudes of children toward clothes.
8. Attitudes of children toward militarism.
9. Attitudes of children toward parents.
10. Attitudes of children toward escape from danger.
11. Special likes and dislikes of children.
12. Miscellaneous differences.

C. *Recreations and Other Activities of Movie and Non-Movie Children.*
D. *Data Bearing on Questions of Interpretation.*

Movie and non-movie groups were compared on each of the above categories and on the numerous subdivisions of each. Differences were computed on no less than 2000 separate items. In Chapter II we report the differences found between the movie and non-movie group on the types of attitudes and conduct tested by the Character Education Inquiry. In Chapters III and IV we report the differences in types of attitudes which were especially tested for this study.

CHAPTER II

DIFFERENCES BETWEEN MOVIE AND NON-MOVIE CHILDREN IN THE TYPES OF CONDUCT AND ATTITUDES WHICH WERE MEASURED BY THE CHARACTER EDUCATION INQUIRY

The Schools in Which the Children Were Tested

OF the school populations tested by the Character Education Inquiry only three were used in this study. These are designated as populations X, Y, and Z.[1] Population X consists of two schools in New Haven, Connecticut, both located in well-to-do, middle-class residential sections of the city; population Y is a consolidated school in the village of Walden, New York; population Z is a school in one of the slum districts of New Haven. These three populations, comprising a total of about nine hundred children, were selected by the Character Education Inquiry as representing a cross-section of the school population of New England cities and small towns.

How These Children Reported Their Movie Attendance

The pupils reported their movie attendance in two different ways. First, they answered a general questionnaire called a "Pupil Data Blank," which contained this question: "How many times a week do you go to the movies?" Second, they reported how they spent their time by filling out a schedule on Monday of one week, Tuesday of the next,

[1] See Hartshorne, Hugh, and May, Mark A., *Studies in the Organization of Character*, New York; The Macmillan Co., 1930, p. 503.

Wednesday of the next, and so on for seven weeks. These time schedules contained records of movie attendance. Since time schedules were available for only a half of the children, the questionnaire data were used for the basic determination of movie attendance supplemented by the time schedule data.

How the Movie and Non-Movie Groups Were Selected

The frequency of attendance at the movies as reported by the children in populations X, Y, and Z is shown in Table II.

TABLE II

FREQUENCY OF ATTENDANCE REPORTED BY ALL CHILDREN, AND BY THE SELECTED MOVIE AND NON-MOVIE GROUPS, IN POPULATIONS X, Y, AND Z

Frequency	Population X			Population Y			Population Z		
	All	M	NM	All	M	NM	All	M	NM
Five or more times a week	3			5	5		12	10	
Four times a week	4	3		4	4		25	23	
Three times a week	14	13		24	24		40	4	
Twice a week	28	3		68	12		67		
Once a week, three per month	106			121			121		20
Once or twice a month	31		7	20		14	3		3
Never, rarely	21		16	35		31	15		10
	207	19	23	277	45	45	283	37	33

M—movie-goers selected for study
NM—non-movie-goers selected for study

The percentages who reported a frequency of attendance of twice a week or more are 23.7, 36.4, and 50.8 for populations X, Y, and Z respectively; the percentages who reported once a week or three times a month are 51.3, 43.6, and 42.8 for X, Y, and Z; the percentage of those who report less than three times a month are 25.0, 20.0, and 6.4, respectively for the populations.

REPUTATION, CONDUCT, AND ATTITUDES 9

In selecting the movie and non-movie groups two criteria were observed. First, only the most extreme cases were selected from *each population*. The wide variation between the populations in the percentages who reported attendance of twice a week or more on the one hand, and those reporting less than three times a month on the other, made it necessary to set the limits of frequency at different points for the different populations. For example, in population Y we included among the movie group 12 children who reported an attendance of twice a week, while in population Z we included among the movie group no children who reported an attendance of twice a week and only four who reported three movies a week (see Table II). While this process leaves the movie groups somewhat unequal in actual frequency of attendance as between communities, yet it has the marked advantage of allowing at the outset for wide community differences in frequency of attendance and insures the selection of only the extreme cases.

The second criterion of selection was that the movie and non-movie children in each population should be equated or alike in respect to such factors as were known to be correlated with the attitudes and conduct which we expected to study. The general procedure which was adopted for this study (that of comparing the attitude of groups contrasted in attendance) required that the two groups be approximately equal in respect to all factors which were correlated both with attendance and with the attitudes and conduct in which the comparisons were to be made. From the results of the Character Education Inquiry we knew at the outset that the attitudes and conduct in which we wished to compare our movie and non-movie groups are correlated moderately [1] with school grade, intelligence,

[1] The coefficients of correlation run from .20 to .60.

age, sex, occupation of father, and cultural background. We accordingly equated our groups in each population for these factors.

Ideally the movie and non-movie groups should be equated for all factors, except movie attendance, which might produce differences in attitudes or in conduct. But no factor can produce a difference in attitudes or conduct between our groups unless it is correlated *both* with attendance and with the attitude or item of conduct in which the comparison is made. From the data of the Character Education Inquiry we knew the factors which are correlated with the attitudes and conduct which we wished to study. But we did not know the factors that are correlated with attendance. This, however, was not serious because such factors must also correlate with attitudes and conduct in order to disturb our results. By equalizing our groups for factors which correlate with attitudes and conduct, not knowing how they correlate with attendance, we were being over-cautious, because some of these factors might not correlate with attendance to an extent that would affect our results.

Using the two criteria just described, the number of children selected for the movie and non-movie groups was as follows:

Population Y	45 movie	45 non-movie
Population XZ	57 movie	56 non-movie
Population XYZ	55 movie boys	42 non-movie boys
Population XYZ	47 movie girls	59 non-movie girls
Population XYZ	102 movie boys and girls	101 non-movie boys and girls

The median attendance of movie groups is three times a week for populations X and Y, and four times a week for Z. The median attendance of the non-movie groups is less than once a month for X and Y and once or twice a month for Z. We estimate that the total movie group attends at least 12 times as often as the non-movie group. Wherever the comparison of the total of 102 movie cases with 101 non-movie cases gives a difference three times as large as its probable error, the four subcomparisons show similar trends. Accordingly, we report only the results from comparing the total movie and non-movie groups.

Differences between Movie and Non-Movie Groups in Reputation

The Character Education Inquiry secured for each child a series of character and personality ratings. These ratings were made both by the teachers and the classmates. They were made mainly on the traits of conduct which were being investigated, namely, honesty, coöperation, self-control, and persistence. The scores were recorded in the categories shown in section A1 of Table I.

Reputation among Teachers

From the teachers were secured for each child four measures of his reputation. These were (1) deportment, (2) school marks, (3) a conduct record, and (4) a check list of character traits. The last two were secured from two different teachers. The conduct record is a rating device, the essential feature of which is that the teacher rates the child's conduct rather than the child himself. The check list of character traits is a list of descriptive adjectives from which the teacher checked for each child those which seemed descriptive of him.[1]

---

[1] For a full description of the conduct record and the check list of character traits and for a discussion of their reliability see *Studies in the Organization of Character, op. cit.*

In Table III we present the differences between the movie and non-movie children in each of the above four measures.

TABLE III

CRITICAL RATIOS SHOWING THE DIFFERENCE BETWEEN MOVIE AND NON-MOVIE GROUPS (OF ALL POPULATIONS) IN REPUTATION AMONG TEACHERS

Reputation	Critical Ratios
Deportment	7.3
School marks	3.8*
Conduct record	1.6
Check lists	3.5

*P.E. difference $= .6745 \sqrt{\sigma_1^2 + \sigma_2^2 - 2r_{12}\sigma_1\sigma_2}$.

All four ratings show differences in favor of the non-movie group. The critical ratios are the differences in mean score divided by the probable error of the differences.[1] That is, the critical ratio of 7.3 in the case of deportment indicates a difference 7.3 times as large as would be apt to occur by chance.

Of the individual measures obtained from teachers, deportment shows the largest difference. Such records being available in all the schools which were studied later, we systematically collected these data. The results are displayed in Table IV. Since deportment records vary in form from school to school we have expressed all of them in terms of sigma deviations, setting the mean deportment of all cases in a given population at zero and the standard deviation at one. This procedure makes the data comparable from population to population and enables us to combine them for all eight populations into final composite scores. Table IV shows that without exception the deportment of non-movie children is superior to that of movie children.

[1] Throughout, with the exception of school marks, probable error of the difference $= .6745 \sqrt{\sigma_1^2 + \sigma_2^2}$.

In only one population, however, is the difference as large as found for the schools studied by the Character Education Inquiry.

TABLE IV

DEPORTMENT RECORDS FOR MOVIE AND NON-MOVIE CASES IN ALL POPULATIONS, SCORES EXPRESSED IN SIGMA DEVIATIONS

	Non-Movie			Movie			Observed Difference
	N	M	S.D.	N	M	S.D.	P.E. Difference
Character Education Inquiry Data	97	.333	.870	100	−.323	1.012	7.3
Troup Junior High, New Haven, Conn.	160	.084	.987	154	−.086	1.003	2.2
Maplewood Junior High, Bridgeport, Conn.	102	.196	1.068	89	−.104	.898	3.1
Roger Ludlow Junior High, Norwalk, Conn.	25	.370	.774	26	−.357	1.065	4.1
Franklin Junior High, Norwalk, Conn.	54	.266	1.036	59	−.252	.968	4.1
Center Junior High, Norwalk, Conn.	38	.193	.971	33	−.217	.971	2.7
Colonel White Junior High, Dayton, Ohio	95	.189	1.012	87	−.172	.947	3.7
Fair Haven Junior High, New Haven, Conn.	132	.230	.915	106	−.303	1.070	6.0
Combination of all populations	703	.2062	.978	654	−.2037	1.0179	11.2

Note: With the exception of Colonel White Junior High, where we were unable to secure intelligence-test scores, the movie and non-movie cases have been equated for age, school grade, sex, socio-economic home background, and either intelligence or educational achievement. For more precise descriptions of these populations see Chapter III. The Troup Junior High cases constitute a preliminary selection and equating which gave too large a number for convenient testing with the attitudes tests. No data are reported in Chapter III on the Maplewood Junior High cases, since the attitudes tests were administered under faulty conditions.

Reputation among Classmates

From classmates three measures of reputation are available. The "Guess Who" test provides two of these measures. This test consists of short descriptions of types of children, and the pupils are asked to guess who the description best fits. After two "buffer" questions there follow twenty-four items such as the following, half indicating "good" and half "bad" characteristics.

> Here is someone who is always ready to play or work with the rest even when he (or she) can't have his own way. Guess who this is.
>
> _____   _____
>
> _____   _____
>
> This is a jolly good fellow—friends with everyone, no matter who they are.
>
> _____   _____
>
> _____   _____

This test is scored by giving a pupil a score of plus one for each appearance of his name in connection with a sentence describing "good" conduct and a score of minus one for each appearance of his name in connection with a sentence describing "bad" conduct. The predicted reliability by the split form method is .95.

On the total score of the "Guess Who" test the non-movie children were rated much higher by their classmates than were the movie children. The difference in favor of the non-movie group is 4.6 times its probable error. On the twelve favorable items of the test the non-movie children were named 24 per cent more often than the movie children, while on the unfavorable items the movie group were named 78 per cent more often. This difference is nearly five times its P.E.

The movie and non-movie groups were compared not only on the total "Guess Who" score but also on each of the 24 items of the test. Complete and usable data were available, however, on 89 movie and 88 non-movie children. For these we counted the number of times a name from each group was mentioned under each of the 24 items.

The movie children were mentioned by their classmates *more frequently* than the non-movie children on the following items:

"This one is always picking on others and annoying them."

"This one is always trying to get by with the least possible trouble and effort to himself."

"This one doesn't obey any rule if he can get out of it."

The non-movie children on the other hand were mentioned more frequently than movie on the following items:

"Here is someone who is kind to younger children, helps them on with their wraps, helps them across the street, etc."

"Here is someone who is always doing little things to make others happy."

"This is someone who is decent and clean in all conversation."

These six items are on the borderline of statistical significance yielding differences from 2.5 to 3.8 times as large as their probable errors. While these differences taken separately are not clearly significant, the fact that the movie group consistently wins three unfavorable and the non-movie three favorable descriptions indicates that these specific differences are genuinely significant.

In addition to using the "Guess Who" test to measure good or bad reputation, we derived a second measure which consisted simply of the number of times a child was named on the test whether under "good" or "bad" descriptions. The movie children were named on the average 26.6 times while the non-movie children were named on the average only 22.7 times, a difference which approaches statistical significance. This indicates that the movie children are better known or that they are more conspicuous among their classmates. At least, their names come more readily to mind.

A third set of scores obtained from classmates hardly measures reputation, but we include it here since its significance is in connection with the two kinds of measures obtained from the "Guess Who" test. This consisted of the number of times each pupil was named by other pupils as one of their "best friends." It measures popularity or conspicuousness or sociability or prestige or simply friendliness. Our expectation here, in the light of the low standing of the movie group on the "Guess Who" test, was that the movie children would be named less frequently by others as best friends. If this were the case the differences on the "Guess Who" test might be explained in part as due to prejudice. Study of the data, however, shows the opposite to be the fact. The movie children were mentioned on the average 2.9 times as best friends, while the non-movie group was mentioned on the average 2.2 times. The difference is 3.3 times as large as its probable error. We thus have a situation in which classmates name the movie children more frequently on all the items of the "Guess Who" test considered as a whole, name them more frequently as best friends, and at the same time give them a generally lower rating in reputation. Clearly the disadvantage of the movie children on the "Guess Who" test cannot be explained in terms of prejudice.

An interesting side light on choices of friends is the proportion who name children of the opposite sex. Six per cent of the non-movie boys and 7.7 per cent of the movie boys name one or more girls among their best friends. The difference is negligible. But 15.2 per cent of the movie girls and 7.4 per cent of the non-movie girls name one or more boys among their best friends. Here twice as many movie as non-movie girls name boys. The difference, however, is not statistically significant.

Reputation for Specific Types of Conduct

The Character Education Inquiry was interested in measuring four types of conduct, coöperation, self-control, persistence, and honesty. The rating scale was accordingly devised to secure opinions from teachers and classmates on these four types of behavior. From the conduct records and check lists which were used by the teachers and from the "Guess Who" test used by the pupils the items pertaining to each of the four types of conduct were combined into reputation scores for coöperation, self-control, persistence, and honesty.

For three of these reputation scores the movie group received an average rating which was lower than the average received by the non-movie group. The significance of these differences in terms of their probable errors were 4.0 for coöperation, 3.4 for self-control, 2.7 for persistence, and .5 for honesty.

Total Reputation Score

The total reputation score used by the Character Education Inquiry consists of the sum of the score of the conduct records, the check lists, deportment grades, and the

"Guess Who" test weighted so as to give pupil opinion equal importance with teacher opinion.

The difference between the movie and non-movie groups in respect to this total score is very marked and in favor of the non-movie group. The difference is 9.4 times its probable error which removes it entirely from the realm of chance. Only 16 per cent of the movie children reach or exceed the median total reputation score of the non-movie group. This difference is one of the largest we have found. It cannot be attributed to prejudiced teachers because the classmates also rate the non-movie children higher. All of our facts point undeniably to the conclusion that this group of 100 children who attended the movies two, three, four and more times a week stand lower in the eyes of their teachers and classmates than the 100 who attend less than once a week.

Differences in Tests of Coöperation

The Character Education Inquiry administered 37 conduct tests in such areas as coöperation, self-control, persistence, and honesty. Five measures of coöperative, or unselfish, or charitable, or altruistic conduct are available. The first two are called the Efficiency Coöperation and Free Choice tests. A competition for an individual and a class prize was announced, to test speed of simple addition. For two minutes every one worked for the individual prize, for two minutes every one worked for the class prize, alternating in this manner for twelve two-minute periods. The difference in amount done for the class and for self constitute a measure of the relative dominance of the group motive. This is the Efficiency Coöperation score. As part of the same exercise seven more units of work were given, except that here each child chose whether to work for the class or for self. The number of units of work sacrificed from his own score to help the class win constitutes the Free Choice test.

Unfortunate children were made the object of charitable behavior in two tests. In the "Kits" test the children were presented with school kits containing pencils, ruler, eraser, etc. They were then invited to share these objects with children who had none. The amount given away was the basis of the score on this test. The other test was a request to bring pictures, jokes, stories, and puzzles to be mounted for hospital children. Four envelopes, one for each type of material, were provided. The score was based on the amount of each type of material turned in. This is the Envelopes test.

A fifth measure of conduct in this area involved both the class group and others. In anticipation of the possibility of receiving a prize in a spelling contest, each class took a straw vote as to what it would do with the money—divide it equally among the class, give it to the one scoring the highest, or buy something for the class, for the school, or for some cause or person in need outside the school. The vote registered the relative dominance of these progressively distant objects in the mind of the subject. This is the Money Vote test.

These five measures were combined into a single score giving somewhat less weight to the Money Vote test than to the others. The figures for this total coöperation score are as follows:

Movie			*Non-Movie*			
N	M	S.D.	N	M	S.D.	P.E.'s
94	110.3	12.97	96	117.3	10.01	6.2

The movie children average slightly over 110 points while the non-movie children average 117 points. The difference in favor of the non-movie children is 6.2 times as large as would tend to occur by chance. This is one of the three largest differences found in the Character Education Inquiry data. Only total reputation and deportment show larger differences.

When the five tests which make up the total service or coöperation score are considered separately, the largest difference appears on the Efficiency Coöperation test. This test more than any other sharpens the conflict between the selfish individual interest and the coöperative group interest. On this test the movie children worked distinctly harder than the non-movie children to win the individual prize, while the non-movie children worked harder than the movie children to win the class prize. The difference is 4.7 times as large as would be apt to occur by chance. Of the data from the Character Education Inquiry, only total reputation, deportment, and total coöperation scores show larger differences.

Next in order of significance is the Envelopes test measuring the number of pictures, puzzles, and jokes brought to school for hospital children. Again the movie children make a poorer showing by a difference 4.1 times its probable error. Consistently on the remaining three tests the movie children are at the disadvantage although the differences are not reliable. Of these the Free Choice and Kits tests give differences 2.8 and 1.8 times as large as would ordinarily be expected by chance. The Money Vote test also shows the movie group as standing lower on the scale than the non-movie group, but in this case the difference is very small, being less than might be expected every other time from the operation of chance alone.

Differences in Tests of Self-Control

Four tests of self-control were employed by the Character Education Inquiry. Two measures involve resistance to the tendency to manipulate objects—a box of puzzles and a safe with a combination lock. One test involves simple addition in the presence of distracting material. A fourth measure consisted of requiring the child to choose between earning a score by monotonous letter counting and breaking open a sealed story to find out how it ended. On the total score, the difference in favor of the non-movie children is 3.6 times as large as its probable error.

Differences in Tests of Persistence

Five tests of persistence are available. Two were derived from the Efficiency Coöperation test, one measuring persistence of the self motive, the other persistence of the class motive. The third and fourth tests measured how long a child would work at a difficult mechanical puzzle and a pencil and paper puzzle. The fifth test measured how long a child would work at disentangling mangled words in order to find out how an interesting story ended. On a combination of these tests there is only the slightest difference, but again in favor of the non-movie group.

Differences in Tests of Honesty

The Character Education Inquiry administered 23 tests of honesty to the children in the three populations from which our movie and non-movie children have been selected. Fourteen of these tests measure schoolroom honesty and nine measure honesty outside of the schoolroom. The essential technique employed in each of these tests is to measure achievement both under conditions which permit cheating and also under conditions which prevent cheating. The excess of the first achievement over the second achievement (allowing for normal gain and variability) measures the amount of deception. We have compared our movie and non-movie cases separately on the school honesty scores and on the out-of-school honesty scores. The following are the figures:

	Movie			Non-Movie			
	N	M	S.D.	N	M	S.D.	P.E.'s
School honesty	76	−13.09	7.80	71	−9.70	7.46	4.1
Out-of-school honesty	62	− 6.75	5.67	73	−6.76	5.90	0.0

As to school honesty there is a large difference once more in favor of the non-movie children, but on the honesty tests which involve out-of-school situations such as taking work home to do, parties, and athletic contests there is no difference whatever. While we do not wish to anticipate possible interpretations of our findings until all the data are reported, it should be remarked that dishonesty in a school system is not evidence of depraved character but is rather a symptom of conflict between the pupil and the teacher or school requirements. These data, accordingly, must be considered in the light of the facts concerning reputation.

Differences between Movie and Non-Movie Groups in Moral Knowledge, Moral Judgments, Social Opinions, and Social Attitude

The Character Education Inquiry administered four batteries of tests which were intended to test in a general way four areas or types of social and moral intelligence.[1]

1. *Moral and Social Information*

This battery consists of five tests which were intended to measure the extent and kinds of information which children have concerning the causes, consequences, relations, and

---

[1] These tests and their statistical properties are described in detail by Hartshorne and May in *Studies in the Organization of Character*, Chapters II and III.

significance of a wide sample of social and moral situations and events.

The average total scores of the movie and non-movie group on this battery of tests were about the same. In so far as these tests measure social and moral information there is no difference between our groups of movie and non-movie children.

2. *Test of Moral Judgment (the Good Citizenship Test)*

This test consists of fifty descriptions of life situations to which the child was asked to respond by checking the answer or solution to each which to him seemed most *sensible, helpful,* and *useful*. The answer to each situation was given a numerical score on a scale of 1 to 5.

The average of the total score of the non-movie children was noticeably higher than the average of the movie group. The difference was 2.5 times its probable error. This is the largest difference that was found between movie and non-movie groups on this general group of tests.

3. *Tests of Social and Moral Opinions (Opinion Ballot A)*

In this series the children expressed their opinions on a wide variety of issues and problems. One series was called a "duties" test. The children were instructed to vote "yes" for each item which expressed a duty to be performed and "no" for each which was not a duty. The average total score of the non-movie group was somewhat higher than the movie group. The difference between the averages, however, was only 1.3 times its probable error.

4. *Tests of Social Attitudes*

This series of tests ran more to preferences, likes, and dislikes, including other types of emotionally toned reactions. It was intended to bring out *feelings* more than any of the others. The test items were selected so as to secure *feeling* responses toward such types of conduct which the Character

Education Inquiry had attempted to measure objectively. These were honesty, coöperation, self-control, and persistence. The tests were set up to answer such questions as this: Does the child have a feeling or a prejudice toward honest or dishonest behavior? If so, is it favorable or unfavorable? How strong is it? The total score, therefore, represents a kind of a net residue of feeling measured so that high scores represent the favorable social attitudes.

The average total score of the non-movie children was again higher than that of the movie group, but not significantly so. The difference was only .6 times as large as its probable error.

Further Analysis of the Character Education Inquiry Attitudes Tests

The differences between movie and non-movie groups which we have just reported are all in terms of averages of total scores. These total scores may be of such a nature that real and significant differences are covered up. The four batteries of tests included a total of 774 items. The responses of the movie and non-movie groups to each of these items were tabulated and compared. This long and laborious process revealed many small differences in the midst of many inconsistencies. Since the number of cases involved is not large all those items (some 99 questions) showing differences two and a half times as large as their probable errors were included in the specially designed attitudes tests which will be described in the following chapter. Of these only eight proved upon further study to show clearly significant differences between movie and non-movie children. To describe all the various types of ethical and moral attitudes which failed to show differences would require many pages. Instead, we refer the interested reader to the tests themselves.

The complete absence of differences indicates rather clearly that movie and non-movie children are essentially alike in their ethical and moral perceptions, judgments, knowledges, attitudes, and opinions. This finding will be confirmed in the next section of our report. The differences which have appeared in the field of attitudes are highly specific and lie outside of the area of the ethical and moral.

Additional Tests

Differences on two more tests administered by the Character Education Inquiry need reporting. The first is the Woodworth-Mathews measure of emotional stability. This consists of a large number of questions tapping many types of emotional disturbances. The movie children confess to more of these, thus indicating greater emotional instability. There is also available the Otis test of suggestibility. Here the difference is essentially zero.

Summary of Findings

We have reported in this chapter the findings from comparing a group of children who go to movies on the average three or four times a week with a group of children who go to movies only once or twice a month. The two groups are alike as to age, school grade, intelligence, occupational level of father, cultural home background, and community. Table V summarizes the significant differences. We have found that the movie children average lower deportment records, do on the average poorer work in their school subjects, are rated lower in reputation by their teachers on two rating forms, are rated lower by their classmates on the "Guess Who" test, are less coöperative and less self-controlled as measured both by ratings and conduct tests, are slightly more deceptive in school situations, are slightly less skillful in judging what is the most useful and helpful and sensible thing to do, and are slightly less emotionally stable. Against this long record, the movie children are superior on only two measures: they are mentioned more frequently on the "Guess Who" test as a whole and are named more frequently as best friends by their classmates. Tests showing no differences also need cataloguing. These include honesty ratings and honesty as measured in out-of-school situations, persistence, suggestibility, and moral knowledge.

TABLE V

PROBABLY SIGNIFICANT DIFFERENCES BETWEEN MOVIE AND NON-MOVIE CHILDREN

Measures	Group Having the Highest Average	Critical Ratios
Deportment	Non-movie	7.3
Scholastic marks	Non-movie	3.8
Teacher ratings, character traits	Non-movie	3.5
Pupil ratings, "Guess Who"	Non-movie	4.6
Reputation for coöperation	Non-movie	4.0
Reputation for self-control	Non-movie	3.4
Total reputation	Non-movie	9.4
Coöperation, total conduct score	Non-movie	6.2
Efficiency Coöperation	Non-movie	4.7
Envelopes Coöperation	Non-movie	4.1
Self-control	Non-movie	3.6
In school honesty	Non-movie	4.1
Named more often on "Guess Who"	Movie	3.5
Named more often as best friends	Movie	3.3

CHAPTER III

PROCEDURES AND ADEQUACY OF THE ATTITUDES TESTS

It has already been said that the Character Education Inquiry data were not collected in the first instance for this study. They, therefore, suffer the inevitable limitations which are encountered when data collected for one purpose are used for another. They never quite fit the conditions of the inquiry. For example, the Character Education Inquiry's moral knowledge and social attitudes tests were not made up in the first place with reference to the types of attitudes which movies are supposed to create. They contain many items, therefore, which lie outside of the present field of inquiry. This may account in part for the negative results. In order to relate the questions and tests which are put to the children more definitely to the content of the films we constructed an entirely new battery of attitudes tests and questionnaires especially designed for the purpose of this study. The story of how these tests were made, the children to whom they were given, and administrative details will be reported in this chapter. The results appear in Chapter IV.

The General Procedure

As already indicated in Chapter II we began by making a detailed analysis of all the attitudes data of the Character Education Inquiry. We tabulated the answers of 102 movie and of 101 non-movie children to each of 774 individual test-questions. From this analysis we formulated certain tentative hypotheses concerning possible spheres of movie influence. These together with suggestions from observation of movies were used as a guide in the construction of the revised tests. These tests were given to movie and non-movie children in Troup Junior High of New Haven, Connecticut, during June of 1929. In the fall of 1929 we formulated a new set of hypotheses and made a second revision of the test. This was given to movie and non-movie groups in Franklin, Center, and Roger Ludlow Junior Highs of Norwalk, Connecticut, in Fair Haven Junior High of New Haven, Connecticut, and in Colonel White Junior High of Dayton, Ohio. While each one of these studies employs essentially the same procedures, minor differences are involved in each. We will save much repetition by describing in this chapter the selection of cases, administrative details, the nature of the tests, and their reliability.

How the Movie and Non-Movie Groups Were Selected

We have already described the selection and equating of 102 movie and of 101 non-movie cases from among those tested by the Character Education Inquiry. In all other populations our first step was to circulate a questionnaire among all children which uniformly contained the following question (see Appendix C).

"How often have you gone to movies (not counting movies during school hours) in the past year? Check on the dotted line *after* the most correct answer. Never been....; Been only a few times....; Go once a month....; Go twice a month....; Go three times a month....; Once a week....; Twice a week ....; Three times a week....; Four times a week....; Five times a week....; Six times a week....."

Procedures and Adequacy of Attitudes Tests 29

Table VI displays the distribution of answers to this question for all of our populations. On the whole 37.7 per cent reported one movie a week, 26.7 per cent reported two or more movies a week, and 35.6 per cent reported less than one movie a week. Troup and Fair Haven Junior High schools are in the city of New Haven, Connecticut, each drawing students from different areas. The nationality backgrounds include all groups with a heavier weighting of Italian. These schools include children from all economic levels except the highest. Franklin, Center, and Roger Ludlow Junior Highs are in the city of Norwalk, Connecticut. Children in Franklin Junior High include a larger proportion with foreign born parents, especially Polish and Italian. Roger Ludlow Junior High includes children from the middle economic levels. Center Junior High has a slightly superior clientele. Colonel White Junior High in Dayton, Ohio, includes children from the middle and upper economic levels with only a small proportion having foreign born parents. Examination of Table VI shows that each community has its distinctive habits of motion-picture attendance.

From each population the preliminary selection of cases included approximately the 10 or 12 per cent who reported that they went most frequently and the 10 or 12 per cent who reported that they went least frequently. In each population the groups were then equated for age, school grade, sex, socio-economic home background and either intelligence or educational achievement as measured by standardized tests.[1] In all populations we excluded Negroes. In all

---

[1] The measure of socio-economic status employed an adaptation of the Sims score card. It asked for occupation of father, ownership of automobile, radio, piano, and Victrola, education of father and mother, language spoken in the home, newspapers and magazines subscribed for, and work outside of the home by the mother. These questions appeared in the questionnaire which included the survey of motion-picture habits. We tested the validity of this measure by comparing the scores of 125 pairs of siblings in the Norwalk schools and obtained a correlation of .86. Neither intelligence nor achievement test scores were available for Dayton children.

Table VI
SUMMARY TABLE OF FREQUENCY OF MOTION-PICTURE ATTENDANCE IN SEVERAL COMMUNITIES

	T	F	RL	C	FH	CW	Total
Five or more times a week	12	2	1	2	8	8	33
Four times a week	12	8	3	2	9	21	55
Three times a week	55	29	9	15	61	74	243
Twice a week	328	95	31	39	204	265	962
Once a week	499	240	105	157	403	421	1825
Three times a month	142	49	43	46	98	110	488
Twice a month	77	40	37	49	106	80	389
Once a month	36	28	20	41	78	51	254
Been only a few times	81	62	27	76	178	92	516
Never been	31	7	3	5	28	4	78
Totals	1273	560	279	432	1173	1126	4843
Per cent two or more times a week	32	24	16	13	24	33	26.7
Per cent once a week	39	43	38	36	34	37	37.7
Per cent less than once a week	29	23	46	51	42	30	35.6

Key to Communities:
  T—Troup Junior High, New Haven, Conn.
  F—Franklin Junior High, Norwalk, Conn.
  RL—Roger Ludlow Junior High, Norwalk, Conn.
  C—Center Junior High, Norwalk, Conn.
  FH—Fair Haven Junior High, New Haven, Conn.
  CW—Colonel White Junior High, Dayton, Ohio.

populations save only Troup Junior High we equated the groups for country of birth of parents. The finally selected cases according to sex and amount of movie attendance for each population are recorded in Table VII. On the whole the movie group averages 2.8 movies a week, while the non-movie group averages only a "few times a year". The contrasts here are definitely greater than in the case of the children selected from the three populations studied by the Character Education Inquiry. If "a few times a year" means once every other month, we estimate that the movie

Procedures and Adequacy of Attitudes Tests

children are exposed to movies on the average about 24 times as much as non-movie children.

Administration of the Tests

A few details about the administration of the tests should be noted. The preliminary questionnaire about movie habits was administered by the home-room teachers who had been

Table VII

FINALLY SELECTED AND EQUATED MOVIE AND NON-MOVIE CASES BY SEX, POPULATION, AND AMOUNT OF ATTENDANCE

	Movie			Non-Movie		
	N	Sex	Average Attendance	N	Sex	Average Attendance
Troup	56	Boys	$3\frac{1}{2}$ per week	54	Boys	Once a month
	50	Girls	$2\frac{1}{2}$ per week	48	Girls	Few times a year
Franklin	28	Boys	$2\frac{3}{4}$ per week	28	Boys	Once a month
	25	Girls	$2\frac{1}{2}$ per week	24	Girls	Few times a year
Center	21	Boys	3 per week	20	Boys	Few times a year
	15	Girls	$2\frac{1}{2}$ per week	18	Girls	Few times a year
Roger Ludlow	12	Boys	$2\frac{1}{2}$ per week	13	Boys	Few times a year
	13	Girls	$2\frac{1}{4}$ per week	12	Girls	Few times a year
Dayton	43	Boys	3 per week	50	Boys	Few times a year
	50	Girls	$2\frac{1}{2}$ per week	45	Girls	Few times a year
Fair Haven	55	Boys	3 per week	65	Boys	Few times a year
	48	Girls	$2\frac{1}{2}$ per week	66	Girls	Few times a year
	416			443		

cautioned to say nothing whatever about its purpose. The attitudes tests were administered two or three weeks later. In Troup Junior High two assembly rooms were available for testing. Admission cards were prepared for the children who were to be tested and these were distributed during the opening home-room period. The movie children were directed to one assembly and the non-movie children to another. No explanation of the purpose of the tests was offered other than that they were being given to selected children in several junior highs. The children were told that taking the tests was not compulsory, *that no names were to be signed*, that they might omit answering any question which they did not want to answer.

Variations in this procedure were made in other schools where it was necessary to test all cases at once in the same room. Here each admission card carried one of six key letters which the children were asked to note on their test papers. This key letter plus a record of their age and sex and the name of their home-room teacher, enabled us not only to identify movie and non-movie cases, but also to determine the name of each child taking each test. Throughout the coöperation of the children was excellent. As far as we could discover no child was aware of the reason for his being asked to take the tests.

How the Tests Were Constructed

The questions and other items which entered into our tests were collected from many sources. First, we included from the Character Education Inquiry tests all the items which offered any promise of revealing differences in further study. Second, we canvassed the literature commending and criticizing the movies for suggestions concerning the types of attitudes, opinions, and ideas which the movies were alleged to create. Third, we received from interested persons, including the research staff of the Payne study group, many suggestions concerning types of attitudes which we should test. Fourth, we observed many movies. From

Procedures and Adequacy of Attitudes Tests

the data drawn from these sources we formulated 29 statements in the form of hypotheses concerning the types of attitudes and opinions on which the movies were alleged to have a direct influence. The test included 329 items and questions, of which 99 were taken from the Character Education Inquiry tests and 230 were invented to test the various hypotheses.

This test was given to 106 movie and 102 non-movie cases in Troup Junior High. Only the barest summary of the findings can be given. The first step in the analysis was to check the classification of the test items under the various hypotheses. Ten persons were given a list of the hypotheses and copies of the test and asked to indicate the hypothesis to which each question applied. Eighty-four per cent of the classifications were as intended when the test was compiled. Our next step was to score the answers to each question and combine the resulting credits according to hypotheses. Out of 25 hypotheses treated in this manner we found that five were reversed, two showed no difference, and 18 were verified or partially verified. Of these 18, however, only two showed clearly reliable differences between movie and non-movie cases. Our third step was to tabulate the answers of the 106 movie and 102 non-movie cases to each of the 329 questions.

The results of this analysis guided a revision and led to a second set of tests. We found that the vocabulary of the first test presented difficulties and that the number of apparently unpromising questions did not warrant further study. The revised test contained all of the 147 questions from the first edition which had shown any tendency to differentiate between the movie and non-movie cases. Again we canvassed the literature, observed movies, read movie reviews, and obtained suggestions from others as to possible differences between movie and non-movie children. These suggestions plus the concrete results already available were formulated into 71 hypotheses. These were grouped into 11 classes and a miscellaneous group. Appendix B displays in detail the complete blue print of hypotheses which were used in preparing the second edition of the tests. In addition to the 147 questions from the first edition, 194 new items were devised. Four persons were asked to classify the test items under their appropriate hypotheses. They classified 92 per cent as intended.

This test was given to 114 movie and 115 non-movie cases in the three junior high schools of Norwalk, Conn., and is reproduced in Appendix C. With minor changes, mostly in the elimination of items which might possibly be offensive to parents, the same test was given to 93 movie and 95 non-movie cases in Dayton, Ohio, and to 103 movie and 131 non-movie children in Fair Haven, Conn.

The Nature and Reliability of the Test

Before presenting the results a word about the nature and reliability of the test is in order. Since we were interested in the net effect of motion-picture attendance on the very wide range of attitudes involved in seventy-one hypotheses, it was necessary that the test take the nature of a questionnaire or survey rather than that of an attitude scale. It aimed to survey many attitudes rather than to measure precisely a single attitude. The questions were cast in the form of ballots on which the children voted, and included true-false questions, multiple-choice questions, and a great variety of other devices.

Three questions may be asked concerning the adequacy of the tests. First, do children record their own sincere opinions and attitudes or do they try to make a good showing by guessing at what they believe their teacher or the examiner approves? We undertook no studies for the purpose of answering this question, but data collected by the Character Education Inquiry shows that children's responses to attitudes questions are to a substantial degree their own independent sincere answers even when their names are signed. Since none of our testing has required children to sign their names and since they were told that they might omit answering any question, the responses with which we have to deal in this study are presumably even closer to sincere and independent attitudes.

Second, how reliable are the responses? Since the test aimed primarily to survey many attitudes, no effort was made to determine its statistical reliability as a whole. Rather, we were interested in the reliability or steadiness of the responses to individual questions. For this purpose we compared answers to questions which were intended to measure the same attitude but which were differently worded and which were widely separated in the tests. For example, we compared the responses to the following two questions:

All Most Many Some Few No Spaniards are love-makers
All Most Many Some Few No Spaniards are too romantic and impractical.

The children were asked to underline one of the six words which best expressed their opinion. There is, of course, no reason for supposing that these two questions should be answered precisely the same way, but for our purpose of discovering whether the movies have created a certain type of attitude or prejudice against Spaniards the two questions were intended to measure the same thing. For 214 children in the Norwalk populations, we found that 68 per cent of the children gave identical responses or shifted their response only one step. Similarly for 12 such pairs of items, we found 72 per cent of the children giving the same or almost the same response. Plotting these responses in the form of a six by six-fold scatter-diagram and correlating the two responses yielded values ranging from .145 to .470 and averaging .346.

Another type of comparison involved such items as the following:

    All   Most   Many   Some   Few   No   Russians are kind and generous.

    Most Russians are kind and generous.   True.   False.

Of those who answered the first question by underlining "All" or "Most" or "Many," 91 per cent answered the second question by underlining "True." Five comparisons of this type gave correlations (biserial) varying from .188 to .586 and averaging .299.

A third type of comparison involved pairs of questions such as:

    Which would you rather be?
        ....A college professor
        ....A cowboy

    Which would you rather be?
        ....A college professor
        ....A popular actor

Of those who checked "a college professor" in the first instance 73 per cent gave the same response in the second instance. In terms of correlations (tetrachoric) four such comparisons gave values ranging from .312 to .900 and averaging .401.

The average of all of these correlations between the re-

Procedures and Adequacy of Attitudes Tests 37

sponses to single test-questions is .345. While such a reliability does not compare favorably with the reliabilities of standardized tests, it should be remembered that the data relate to single test-questions and that several test-questions have been directed toward each attitude. That such reliabilities are adequate for the purpose of distinguishing contrasted groups is shown by the fact that the Efficiency Coöperation test, which yielded one of the largest differences of the Character Education Inquiry tests, correlates on the average only .25 with the other tests of coöperation.

Third, is the testing procedure sufficiently sensitive to register different attitudes? We have just shown that children tend to give the same responses to similar questions. Do they give different responses to questions which are only superficially alike? In order to determine whether changing only a few words would alter the responses we compared the following two questions.

> Mike was the captain of a ship in the South Seas. He fell in love with a girl in a dance hall. He wanted her to go to sea with him but she refused. What is most likely to happen?
> ....Mike cursed his bad luck and went back to his ship without her.
> ....Mike and his crew smashed the lamps in the dance hall and in the confusion carried the girl off by force.

> Mike was the captain of a ship in the South Seas. A girl in a dance hall made love to him, but when Mike wanted her to go to sea with him she refused. What should Mike do?
> ....Curse his bad luck and go back to his ship without her.
> ....Smash the lamps in the dance hall and carry the girl off by force.

Of 219 children answering these questions 168 said in the first instance that Mike was likely to go back to his ship without the girl. All but eight of these 168 children in the second instance completely reversed themselves and said that Mike should carry off the girl by force. In terms of correlations (tetrachoric) the association between the responses to the two test items is very highly negative, $-.84$. That is, two questions which are only superficially alike induced radically different responses. The first question yielded one of the largest differences between movie and non-movie cases, the second showed no difference whatever.

Summary; Adequacy of the Procedure

We have described in this chapter the methods of selecting movie and non-movie children, administrative details, the nature of the tests, and their validity, reliability, and sensitivity. Taken together, these data provide the basis for a judgment of the adequacy of the whole procedure. As far as the tests are concerned it may be said that they elicit responses which are sincere and independent, which are sufficiently reliable, and which are sensitive to genuine changes in the test elements even though the changes involve but a few words. Such tests might be inadequate for the purpose of discovering differences in the attitudes of 50 children who go to movies once a week and 50 children who go twice a week, but they are quite adequate for the purpose of discovering differences in the attitudes of 300 children who go to movies nearly three times a week and 300 children who go to movies less than once a month.

CHAPTER IV

RESULTS OF THE ATTITUDES SURVEY

WE shall report the findings from the attitude tests according to the list of hypotheses which guided their construction. These fall into eleven groups such as attitudes toward the heroes and "boobs" of the movies, toward people of other lands, prohibition, crime, etc. Appendix B displays the complete list of hypotheses. In the appendix these hypotheses are given as originally formulated. Here we restate the hypotheses in terms of the actual results which we have found.

1. *The Heroes and Boobs of the Movies*

Our first group of hypotheses centers around the supposed tendency of the movies to place certain characters in a favorable light and to hold up others to ridicule. In particular, it has been charged that criminals, gang leaders, rum runners, athletes, cowboys, chorus girls, and actors are held up to admiration in the movies while prohibition agents, policemen, detectives, Protestant ministers, college professors, and social workers are made to appear incompetent, lazy, foolish, or lacking in intelligence. We have tried to catch the special flavor or halo or characteristics which the movies throw around these types and to determine whether the attitudes of frequent movie attenders conform with those suggested by the pictures and at the same time differ from the attitudes of infrequent movie attenders.

40 SOCIAL CONDUCT AND ATTITUDES OF MOVIE FANS

Under the general heading of Heroes and "Boobs" of the movies we present results from twelve specific formulations of hypotheses designed to test this point. For convenience, we have placed attitudes toward criminals, gang leaders, and rum runners under the general heading of crime and criminals, and attitudes toward prohibition agents and supporters of prohibition under the heading of prohibition.

One of the most significant differences which we have found anywhere in our studies is in the answers to the following question:

Which would you rather be? Check one.
.... A college professor
.... A popular actor

On the whole the movie children check "A popular actor" much more frequently than do non-movie children, and conversely non-movie children check "A college professor" much more frequently than do movie children. As an illustration of our findings Table VIII presents the complete data showing the per cent of children giving these two answers. All together we have fifteen subcomparisons. Although, with one exception, all comparisons show the same tendency there are exceptionally large variations between movie and non-movie cases. In Troup and Norwalk schools the difference between the replies of movie and non-movie cases is only 10 per cent, in Dayton the difference is 50 per cent, and between Dayton movie and non-movie girls it is 60 per cent. Clearly the kind of community to which a child belongs has something to do with the differences in the attitudes of movie and non-movie children. In combining the data for the several populations we elected to include the data from Troup Junior High, although this

TABLE VIII

PERCENTAGE OF MOVIE AND NON-MOVIE CHILDREN BY SEX AND POPULATION CHECKING "A COLLEGE PROFESSOR" OR "A POPULAR ACTOR" IN RESPONSE TO THE QUESTION "WHICH WOULD YOU RATHER BE?"

Populations	Movie or Non-Movie	Sex	N	Percentages	
				College Professor	Popular Actor
Troup Junior High	Non-movie	Boys	50	72	28
	Movie	Boys	51	51	49
	Non-movie	Girls	49	59	41
	Movie	Girls	50	58	42
	Non-movie	B & G	99	66	34
	Movie	B & G	101	55	45
Norwalk Junior Highs	Non-movie	Boys	60	67	33
	Movie	Boys	59	68	32
	Non-movie	Girls	55	65	35
	Movie	Girls	51	41	59
	Non-movie	B & G	115	66	34
	Movie	B & G	110	55	45
Fair Haven Junior High	Non-movie	Boys	63	84	16
	Movie	Boys	54	57	43
	Non-movie	Girls	61	64	36
	Movie	Girls	48	56	44
	Non-movie	B & G	124	74	26
	Movie	B & G	102	58	44
Colonel White Junior High	Non-movie	Boys	48	62	38
	Movie	Boys	41	27	73
	Non-movie	Girls	43	79	21
	Movie	Girls	54	15	85
	Non-movie	B & G	91	70	30
	Movie	B & G	95	20	80
Four populations combined	Non-movie	Boys	221	72.0	28.0
	Movie	Boys	205	52.7	47.3
	Non-movie	Girls	208	66.4	33.6
	Movie	Girls	203	41.8	58.2
	Non-movie	B & G	429	69.2	30.8
	Movie	B & G	408	47.3	52.7

tends slightly to exaggerate the differences. On the final combined comparison 408 movie and 429 non-movie children have been used. Of the movie cases 52.7 per cent check "A popular actor," while only 30.8 per cent of the non-movie cases give this response. Conversely, 47.3 per cent of the movie and 69.2 per cent of the non-movie check "A college professor." The difference of 21.9 per cent is more than nine times as large a difference as would be apt to occur by chance.

A question showing a similar difference is this one:

Which would you rather be? (NFD, 4.2 P.E.)
(a) .... a college professor   (NMG)
(b) .... a cowboy   (MG)

Here and in all subsequent comparisons we shall indicate the essential facts by key letters. The symbols NFD indicate that this question was submitted to Norwalk, Fair Haven, and Dayton children. The letters NMG indicate that the non-movie girls checked the answer "A college professor," while MG indicates that the movie girls tended to check "A cowboy." The figures 4.2 P.E. indicate that the difference is 4.2 times as large as its probable error. In terms of actual percentages 68.4 per cent of 139 movie girls and 83.0 per cent of 153 non-movie girls checked "a college professor." The movie and non-movie boys show the same tendency but here the differences are so small as to be unreliable.

Another question approaching attitudes toward college professors is the following: [1]

All <u>Most Many</u> Some Few No   college professors are strong, robust men. (NFD 5.5 P.E.)

[1] In reporting these differences the order from left to right is All Most Many Some Few No. In the tests, half of the questions appeared in the order No Few Some Many Most All.

Here the children were asked to underline the one of the six words which best expressed their opinion about college professors. The question was given to Norwalk, Fair Haven, and Dayton children. The single underlining indicates that the movie children tended to say that "some" or "few" or "no" college professors are strong, robust men while the double underlining indicates that non-movie children tended to say that "most" or "many" college professors are strong, robust men. The difference is more than five times as large as its probable error. As a final illustration of the details behind this summary we give the following percentages of responses under each of the six words:[1]

	All	Most	Many	Some	Few	No
Non-Movie	4.3	15.7	20.6	39.3	17.2	3.1
Movie	4.7	12.0	11.0	42.7	24.7	5.0

All together 72.4 per cent of the movie and 59.6 per cent of the non-movie cases responded "some" or "few" or "no," while 23.0 per cent of the movie and 31.3 per cent of the non-movie responded "most" or "many."

Besides these three questions must be placed three more which failed to show differences. These are the following:

All	Most	Many	Some	Few	No	college professors could do well in business if they wanted to.
All	Most	Many	Some	Few	No	college professors are sickly, weak men who have to wear glasses.
All	Most	Many	Some	Few	No	college professors are most impractical.

[1] Detailed data on twenty items appear in Appendix D.

Since the single test items are not highly reliable, we do not regard the failures of these items to show differences as contradicting the differences already reported.

Closely akin to this tendency are answers to the question:

> Which of the following people would you like to know more about? (TNFD, 9.7 P.E.)
> .... Helen Hunter, who is just beginning her medical training (NM)
> .... Sally O'Dare, who is just getting her first chance in a Broadway show (M)

This question was given to all four populations and throughout the movie children check Sally O'Dare more frequently than the non-movie children. The difference here is 22.4 per cent or nearly ten times as large as its probable error.

To the same effect are the following:

All Most Many <u>Some</u> <u>Few</u> No dancers had fascinating lines. (TNFD, 4.1 P.E.)

<u>All Most Many</u> Some <u>Few</u> No professional dancers are decent folk. (NFD, 3.3 P.E.)

However, when the question is "All Most Many Some Few No chorus girls are to be admired" or "All Most Many Some Few No chorus girls lead shady lives" no differences appear. Next, consider the following:

<u>All Most Many</u> Some <u>Few No</u> chorus girls are worth while members of society. (TNFD, 6.4 P.E.)

Here we find the non-movie children approving the chorus girl. Further, the tendency is consistent through all the populations and for both sexes and is one of the eleven most reliable differences which we have found. Evidently admiration of and interest in the popular actor, the dancer, and Sally O'Dare on the part of the movie children does not necessarily mean that movie children will show approval of them.

That admiration of and interest in a type by the movie children does not mean approval is indicated by responses to questions designed to test attitudes toward cowboys. One question failed to show a difference while two give the following contrasts:

All	Most	<u>Many</u>	<u>Some</u>	Few	<u>No</u>	cowboys are heavy drinkers. (NFD, girls 4.3 P.E.)
All	Most	Many	<u>Some</u>	Few	<u>No</u>	cowboys are dirty, mean, and lazy. (NFD, 5.5 P.E.)

For both of these questions the non-movie group divides itself into two camps, one approving and the other disapproving. The movie children take a middle ground tending to say that some cowboys are heavy drinkers and a few are dirty, mean, and lazy.

Eight questions were inserted in the tests to sample attitudes toward policemen and toward small-town police and detectives. Only one of these shows a difference.

<u>All</u>	<u>Most</u>	<u>Many</u>	<u>Some</u>	Few	No	policemen torture and mistreat anyone suspected of a crime. (NFD, 4.0 P.E.)

The movie children tend to say that "All" or "Most" or "Many" policemen torture and mistreat anyone suspected of a crime. There is a slight tendency for the movie children to say that "Few" or "No" small-town police officials are clever and efficient. The remaining items which show no difference characterize policemen and detectives as "rough and bullying," as "ridiculous and boastful fellows," as "courteous and well intentioned," as being unable "to follow a clue if it were shown to them."

Three items in the tests characterized social workers and reformers as "meddlers," as "busybodies," and as having "the best interests of every one at heart." Only one of these showed a difference.

<u>All</u> <u>Most</u> Many Some Few No   social workers are busybodies. (NFD Boys, 4.9 P.E.)

Contrary to our expectations, the movie children tend to deny that social workers are busybodies.

Protestant ministers were characterized in two test-questions as "highly intelligent" and as "below average intelligence." Only the first showed a difference.

All <u>Most</u> <u>Many</u> <u>Some</u> Few No   Protestant ministers are highly intelligent. (TNFD, 4.2 P.E.)

Again the result was contrary to our expectations, the movie children tending to say that "All" or "Most" Protestant ministers are highly intelligent.

Prize fighters, athletes, and sea captains were variously described in the test as "loyal and true," "brave," "unworthy of anyone's admiration," "to be admired," and as caring "little about the game." None of the seven items of this type showed differences.

In summary of these differences we have found that the movie children admire, or are more interested in, or want to know more about, cowboys, popular actors, dancers, and chorus girls, without necessarily approving them. The non-movie children tend to be more interested in the college professor and young medical student. Contrary to our expectations, the movie children think well of social workers and Protestant ministers. The movie children tend to believe that policemen torture and mistreat those suspected of a crime. No differences appeared in the attitudes toward sea captains, prize fighters, or athletes.

2. *The Peoples of Other Lands*

A second general criticism of the movies is that they present the people of other lands in an unfavorable light. In particular, it is charged that Chinese and Mexicans seem persistently to be cast in the rôle of villain, Spaniards in the rôle of love-maker, etc. Does the constant repetition of such types change the attitudes of movie children toward these groups? Questions designed to test attitudes toward Mexicans, Japanese, and Italians failed to show differences. Fourteen questions were employed. Mexicans were characterized as "dirty, evil looking fellows," "upright citizens and honest men," "civilized," "half-breeds," and as "bandits." Japanese were described in the questions as "desirable citizens for the United States," as readily becoming "the tools of criminal gangs," as persons who "should be kept out of the United States," and as "rich men's servants." Italians were characterized as "quick to repay injury with revenge," as "the tools of criminal gangs," and as "desirable citizens for the United States."

Of twenty test-questions designed to measure attitudes toward Frenchmen, Spaniards, Chinese, Arabs, and Russians, we have reliable differences on six of the following items:

All	Most	Many	Some	Few	No	Frenchmen are romantic love-makers. (NFD Boys, 4.0 P.E.)

48   SOCIAL CONDUCT AND ATTITUDES OF MOVIE FANS

| All | Most | Many | Some | Few | No | Arab chieftains are fierce fighters. (NFD, 4.3 P.E.) |

Most Arab chieftains are handsome men, hard riders, and fierce fighters. (TNFD Girls, 4.8 P.E.)   <u>True</u>,   <u>False</u>.

All	Most	Many	Some	Few	No	Chinese readily become the tools of criminal gangs. (NFD Boys, 4.5 P.E)
All	Most	Many	Some	Few	No	Spaniards are romantic and impractical. (NFD Boys, 4.0 P.E.)
All	Most	Many	Some	Few	No	Spaniards are lovemakers. (TNFD, 3.2 P.E.)
All	Most	Many	Some	Few	No	Russians are kind and generous. (TNFD, 5.0 P.E.)

Additional items characterizing these groups in various ways showed no differences. Of the seven items quoted one is contrary to expectations suggested by critics of the movies, two are self-contradictory, and one is inconsistent. It is the non-movie rather than the movie children who tend to say that Frenchmen are romantic love-makers. In the case of Arabs, the non-movie children begin by saying that "All" or "Most" Arab chieftains are fierce fighters and end by replying "False" to the statement that "Most Arab chieftains are handsome men, hard riders, and fierce fighters." The responses to the question concerning Chinese are inconsistent, the non-movie cases tending to respond "Many" while the movie cases tend to respond "Most" as well as "Few" and "No." To balance these, we have two

Results of the Attitudes Survey 49

consistent differences, the second of which is not reliable showing that the movie children believe that "All" or "Most" or "Many" Spaniards are "romantic and impractical" or "love-makers." There is also a tendency for the movie children to say that few Russians are kind and generous.

Of the thirty-four questions designed to test the general hypothesis that the movies develop specific antipathies toward the people of other lands only three show meaningful and reliable differences, and one of these is contrary to expectations of those critical of the movie influence.

3. *Prohibition*

Evidently the constant repetition of scenes portraying the use of liquor on the motion-picture screen has made its mark on the opinions of the movie children. Consider the following differences:

All Most <u>Many</u> Some Few No — adult men of this country have been drunk one or more times since the passage of the prohibition amendment. (NF, 5.3 P.E.)

All Most Many <u>Some</u> Few No — modern parties are complete without wine to drink. (TNFD, 5.0 P.E.)

All Most Many <u>Some</u> Few No — football games are occasions at which many people get drunk. (TNFD, 4.0 P.E.)

Few people get drunk at football games these days. (NF, 3.2 P.E.) <u>True</u>, False.

50 Social Conduct and Attitudes of Movie Fans

<u>All</u> <u>Most</u> <u>Many</u> Some Few No supporters of prohibition have the welfare of the whole country at heart. (TNFD, 6.3 P.E.)

<u>All</u> <u>Most</u> <u>Many</u> Some Few No people who vote dry practice what they vote. (TNFD Girls, 4.1 P.E.)

It is no one's business if a reputable citizen takes an occasional drink. (TNF Girls, 4.7 P.E.) <u>True</u>, False.

According to these items the movie children tend to say that most men have been drunk one or more times, that few modern parties are complete without something to drink, that many people get drunk at most football games, that few supporters of prohibition are sincere, and that a respectable citizen may take an occasional drink if he wishes to. The seven items are all those, from among twenty-seven, which show reliable or nearly reliable differences. The first four items indicate that the movie children tend to believe that excessive drinking is rather common. Such a belief might readily follow from the frequency with which drinking is presented on the motion-picture screen. The important criticism of the movies which has been advanced, however, is not that drinking appears but that the effect is to weaken support for a worthy experiment in social engineering. To test this point, questions were specifically designed to test attitudes toward the desirability of modification or enforcement and toward the social values or shortcomings of prohibition. The test given to children in Troup Junior High included thirteen questions of this type. Only two of these showed any tendency to differentiate the movie and non-movie cases and these two on further trial showed no difference in the Norwalk, Fairhaven, or Dayton populations. An additional four questions designed to test which group was more concerned with the social consequences and which more concerned with the restrictions upon the individual which prohibition has enforced also show no differences.

4. *Crime and Criminals*

A perplexing social problem which seems to defy solution usually results in not a few putting the blame on the home, or the school, or the church, or the movies. The prevalence of crime pictures lends color to the feeling of many that the movies are responsible in part. The criminal is more often than not cast in the rôle of hero with many desirable qualities. To be sure the crime itself is never approved and contrary to real life the criminal always reforms or is punished. Does the constant rôle of hero give the frequent movie attender the idea that the criminal is brave, kind, and generous in his way, and clever and intelligent? Does the uniformity with which the criminal gets punished, as urged by friends of the movies, make any impression on the child? Or does the frequency with which the criminal reforms make the stronger impression? We directed eighteen test elements to the first question, five to the second, and five to the third.

The eighteen test items characterize gang leaders, criminals, thieves, robbers, and rum runners in many ways. They are "real men," "usually fine looking fellows with good manners and generous ways," "brave dare-devil fellows out for adventure," "courageous, brave, and nervy," "cowards in the face of danger," "chivalrous and tenderhearted toward women and children," "honorable in their dealings with their own kind," and "clever enough to make a good living honestly if they wanted to." Of all these items only one shows a reliable difference and that appears between the movie girls and non-movie girls. Twenty-one per cent of the non-movie girls and only 10 per cent of the movie girls say that "All" gang leaders are real men. This single difference is contrary to expectations created by the tendency of the gang leaders to be cast in the rôle of hero.

Among the five items testing children's opinions about how frequently criminals escape punishment, one clear difference appears. This is to the following question:

<u>All Most Many Some</u> Few No criminals when sentenced to death escape with last-minute pardons. (TNFD, 4.9 P.E.)

Here we find the movie children saying that few or no criminals escape with last-minute pardons. A difference which is not clearly reliable indicates that the movie children tend to say that "No" murderers escape their just punishment.

Of five test-questions designed to determine whether the movie children have the idea that the criminal can escape by reforming, none show even a slight tendency to differentiate the movie and non-movie cases.

5. *Sex Attitudes*

Although a study of possible differences between the attitudes of movie and non-movie children toward sex presented not a few dangers especially when approached though written questions in the public schools, we thought the problem of sufficient importance to warrant a trial. It was, of course, impossible to aim questions directly at sex attitudes

RESULTS OF THE ATTITUDES SURVEY 53

and we have been compelled to "beat about the bush," so to speak, and be content with what we could get. In every case what we could get was determined by the good judgment of the superintendents of our various schools as to the sensitivity of their constituencies.

One question asked was, "How soon should a girl begin to think of getting married?" This was repeated for boys. Three answers were supplied, such as "Before she is twenty-one," "Between twenty-one and twenty-five," and "After twenty-five." Our hypothesis was that the movie children would tend to check earlier years. The responses from two schools, however, showed not the least difference.

We explored opinions about the general success or failure of marriage by such questions as "All Most Many Some Few No" "husbands buy little presents for their wives occasionally," "husbands and wives quarrel all the time," and "marriages are successful." None of these questions yielded a significant difference. One of the questions given to the movie and non-movie cases in Troup Junior High read "All Most Many Some Few No marriages are unsuccessful if the man is unable to earn a decent wage." Here the movie children tended to respond "All" or "Most" or "Many." The same tendency appeared from the Norwalk cases, making the difference reliable, but further testing in Fair Haven and Dayton showed precisely the opposite tendency. Three more items suggested by the difference found in Troup Junior High were inserted and these also failed to differentiate the movie and non-movie cases.

We attempted to get at sex attitudes indirectly by presenting a list of ten offenses and asking the children to check the three worst ones. Such items as "swearing," "stealing," "telling smutty stories," "fist fighting," etc., were included. No difference appeared in the frequency with which these offenses were checked by the movie and non-movie groups.

A variation of this consisted of four check lists of offenders. A sample of one of these is as follows:

> Below are short descriptions of Junior High School girls whom you may know. Check the *two* whom you most dislike.
> ...... Boy crazy.
> ...... Is proud of the fact that she dares to smoke cigarettes.
> ...... The class giggler, she laughs and giggles at everything.
> ...... The innocent one, so ignorant of the world that she is always asking foolish questions.

In each case we tried to frame descriptions which would elicit one response from the movie and another response from non-movie children. We expected, for example, that the supposedly more sophisticated movie children would tend to check the "giggler" and the "innocent one." One set of such questions was given in Norwalk and three in Dayton and Fair Haven. No differences on any of these questions appeared.

Three sets of questions were designed to get at reasons for continuing or not continuing to go with some one of the opposite sex. Of these, the following yielded three significant differences.

> When is a girl justified in throwing over her best fellow? In the following list check the two best reasons for a girl refusing to go any more with a boy.
> (a) ...... When he gets serious and wants to marry her.
> (b) ...... When he proves that he can't hold a job of any kind.
> (c) ...... When he wants to kiss her good night.
> (d) ...... When he gets angry and scolds.
> (e) ...... When he is too free in making love to other girls.

This question was given to Norwalk and Fair Haven children. Fifty-two per cent of the movie boys and 69 per cent of the non-movie boys checked "When he proves that he can't hold a job of any kind." The tendency, however, was completely reversed by the girls. Both differences are reliable being four and four-and-a-half times as large as would be expected by chance. Such a contrast should give pause to anyone who imagines that the influence of movies is simple and direct in changing children's attitudes. Item (d), "When he wants to kiss her good night" also yields a reliable difference, in this case, between the two groups of girls. Only 2 per cent of the movie girls check this as a good reason while 14 per cent of the non-movie girls check this reason. Beside this difference should be placed one in answer to item (e) which falls barely short of being reliable. Eighty-two per cent of the movie girls and only 67 per cent of the non-movie girls check "When he is too free in making love to other girls."

Still another device might have been included under the heading of crime and criminals. A sample is as follows:

> Joe Henderson was a well educated and cultured man who had had hard luck. He had sunk to the level of running a dance hall in Chinatown and grew so powerful that he could order a man shot at will. He suddenly closed up his dance hall and went straight. What is the most probable reason for his sudden change? (TNFD, 6.2 P.E.)
> (a) ..(NM)..He was afraid that eventually the police would find him out and send him to prison.
> (b) ... (M)..He fell in love with a girl who made him see what kind of a life he was living.

Seventy-six per cent of the movie and only 63 per cent of the non-movie checked item (b) as most probable. This question was given in all four schools. The difference is more than six times as large as its probable error. One other item of this type was included, and it also showed a difference more than six times as large as its probable error.

Scar-faced Johnson had led a criminal career all his life. He suddenly quit the game and went straight. What is the most probable explanation of his sudden change? (NFD, 6.2 P.E.)

(a) .. (NM).. He was afraid the police would eventually get him.

(b) ... (M).. He fell in love with a girl who insisted that he go straight.

Seventy-five per cent of the movie and only 59 per cent of the non-movie children checked the second answer. Evidently the movie children believe in the efficiency of feminine charms or the story of the reform of the villain carries irresistible appeal.

Somewhat akin to this type of difference is another which also involves probability.

Mike was the captain of a ship in the South Seas. He fell in love with a girl in a dance hall. He wanted her to go to sea with him, but she refused. What is most likely to happen? (TNFD, 7.2 P.E.)

(a) ..(NM)..Mike cursed his bad luck and went back to his ship without her.

(b) ... (M).. Mike and his crew smashed the lamps in the dance hall and in the confusion carried the girl off by force.

Forty-nine per cent of the movie and 33 per cent of the non-movie children guess that Mike and his crew will carry the girl off by force. The difference is more than seven times as large as its probable error. Another short story of this type about "John Hunter, the leading athlete and ladies' man of the senior class" showed a similar though not reliable difference. "At a dance in a neighboring town a girl made eyes at him, but when John asked her to dance with him, she refused. What is John most likely to do?" The movie children tend to say "Compel her to dance with him anyway" while the non-movie say "Leave her alone." However, when these two questions were varied asking "What *should* Mike do?" and "What *should* John do?" no difference appeared.

In summary of these rather miscellaneous questions we have no consistent differences in attitudes toward marriage and toward offenses. Reasons for continuing to go with a person of the opposite sex give contradictory results. Three items which are in answer to the question "What is most likely to happen?" show reliable and consistent tendencies. The movie children believe that the love of a woman is more apt to lead to reform than fear of the police. When a short story is presented they expect the hero to "carry the girl off by force" or to "compel her to dance with him anyway," but, when approval or disapproval of such action is asked, no difference appears.

6. *Attitudes toward School*

The attitude tests of the Character Education Inquiry contained a dozen questions sampling attitudes toward school. Rather suggestive differences appeared, but further study reveals only two two clearly reliable differences.

All	Most	Many	Some	Few	No	
All	Most	Many	Some	Few	No	teachers are too easy with their pupils. (TNFD, 4.9 P.E.)
All	Most	Many	Some	Few	No	schoolbooks are interesting. (TNFD, 5.0 P.E.)

The movie children tend to say that "Few" teachers are too easy with their pupils and that "Many" or "Some" or "Few" or "No" schoolbooks are interesting. Unreliable differences to the same effect show that the movie children tend to say that "All" or "Most" or "Many" teachers are too hard with their pupils and that "All" or "Most" school readers are full of dull stories.

7. *Clothing*

A minor element in six questions in the attitudes tests of the Character Education Inquiry concerned clothes. Three of these showed possibly significant differences. Following our policy of subjecting each clue to more careful study we constructed test questions which made the attitudes toward clothing the central instead of a minor element in the question. The final revision of the tests contained eleven test elements of which four show clearly reliable differences and one probably reliable difference.

A little rouge, high heels, and smart clothes add to the attractiveness of a girl. (TNFD, 6.8 P.E.) True. False.

Good clothes help to make the man. (TNFD, 6.4 P.E.) True. False.

All Most Many Some Few No children would stay away from a party rather than wear shabby clothes. (NFD, 5.2 P.E.)

All Most Many Some Few No attractive girls wear smart clothes. (NFD, 3.3 P.E.)

The trend of the answers is consistent. The movie children tend to say that "A little rouge, high heels, and smart clothes add to the attractiveness of a girl," that "Good clothes help to make the man," and that "All" or "Most" "smartly dressed girls are popular," "attractive girls wear smart clothes," "children would stay away from a party rather than wear shabby clothes."

8. *Militarism*

It has been charged that through certain types of pictures and especially newsreels the movies tend to glorify the soldier, the army, and war itself. The first revision of our tests contained eight questions of which only three showed the slightest differences. These were retained and seven more questions added to the final revision. None of the ten questions show even a slight tendency to differentiate the movie and non-movie groups. Samples of these questions are as follows:

> The nation with a large military force will be tempted to use it. True. False.
> Marching should thrill every heart. True. False.
> All Most Many Some Few No differences between nations can be settled by peaceful methods.

9. *Parental Attitudes*

Much has been written about the forces which are disintegrating family life. Many have felt that frequent movie-going by the child is particularly disruptive. The mere absence from the home several nights a week is not the only factor. Parents who permit their children only a very occasional movie seem to make the assumption that several movies a week means an undue independence if not defiance of parental wishes. In the investigation of children's attitudes toward their parents we used three types of questions. In the first a list such as "to smoke," "to visit a friend," "to go to a football game in a neighboring town" were presented and the children were asked to check the things which they should get permission to do. Our expectation when we first tried this procedure with a list of twenty items in Troup Junior High was that the movie children would check fewer things. Counting the number of checks, however, showed no difference. We then studied the number of checks for each of the twenty items. It appeared that the movie children tended to check the activities for which parental approval seemed more necessary, while the non-movie children tended to check activities for which parental approval seemed hardly necessary.

In the second revision thirteen more items were added to this check list. A study of each individual item showed only two reliable differences. The movie children tended to say that it was not necessary to obtain parental permission "to visit a friend" or "to visit a neighbor." Our next step was to select the ten items checked most frequently by all children and the ten checked least frequently. The first list consisted of things which more than 60 per cent of all children thought they should get parental approval to do. Such things as "to go with the school football team to another town," "to take the basket-ball team to another town in the family car," and "to go to visit a distant friend" are included here. The second list consisted of things which the majority of children thought might be done without asking permission. This list includes such things as "to stay after school half an hour," "to read a novel," and "to give your own money to the Red Cross." We scored the list of thirty-three items by giving a credit of plus one for every check before the ten items most frequently checked by all children and a credit of minus one for every check before the ten items least frequently checked by all children. The resulting scores give the movie children in Norwalk, Fair Haven, and Dayton the distinct advantage over non-movie children. Almost all of the difference, however, is supplied by the girls, the movie girls achieving higher scores by a difference more than six times as large as its probable error.

Contrary to expectations, it is the movie children, and especially the movie girls, who are more sensitive to parental approvals and disapprovals.

The second procedure which was used to elicit parental attitudes required the children to check all the sources of disagreement with parents out of a list of ten possible sources. Here we studied each individual source of disagreement and scored the whole question by counting the number of things checked. The following is a complete list of the sources of disagreement with indications of which group checked each source most frequently.

>Use of the family automobile. (7.5 P.E. MB)
>The boys or girls you choose as your friends. (5.5. P.E. MG)
>Your spending money.
>Number of times you are out on school nights. (3.9 P.E. M)
>Your school grades.
>The hour you get in at night. (3.9 P.E. M)
>Home duties (tending furnaces, washing dishes).
>The way you dress.
>Smoking.
>Your dates.

With the single exception of home duties the movie children check these sources of disagreement more frequently. The movie children check the use of the family automobile and the choice of friends more frequently by highly reliable differences. When the list is scored by counting the number of checks, the movie children acknowledge on the average 2.91 and the non-movie 2.46 sources of disagreement. This difference approaches reliability, being 3.5 times as large as its probable error.

Still a third method of obtaining parental attitudes was to ask the question "What are the desirable traits in a father?" and "What are the desirable traits in a mother?"

Under each question six answers were given and the children were asked to check the two most desirable traits. Such items as "being a college graduate," "making plenty of money," "owning a good-looking car," and "being prominent in social life" were listed. Of the twelve traits only one showed a reliable difference. The movie girls checked "never nagging his children about what they do" more frequently than non-movie girls as a desirable trait in a father. No difference appeared for boys and a similar trait for mothers showed no difference.

These findings are difficult of interpretation. That movie girls say "not nagging" is a most desirable trait in a father and that both movie boys and movie girls check more sources of disagreement may be interpreted as evidence of friction between them and their parents. But this interpretation will hardly square with the fact that movie children check as many things for which permission should be obtained and the fact that they are more discriminating in their checking. As plausible an interpretation would be that movie children are more discriminating and more sensitive to parental approvals and disapprovals.

10. *Escape from Threatening Danger*

The escape of the hero from situations threatening danger is one of the most common motifs of the movies. The following are samples of the four items inserted to test this point.

> Tom Larson was a wealthy Arizona ranch owner. He had been losing cattle and suspected cattle rustling. While investigating the loss of his cattle, he found himself surrounded by bandits. The bandits locked him up in an abandoned mine and told him that within a week his cattle would be driven across the border. What is most likely to happen? (TNFD, 5.7 P.E.)

(M) Tom finds a secret exit from the mine, gathers a posse, and captures the bandits just as they are about to cross the border.

(NM) Tom is unable to escape in time and loses all his cattle.

Dick and Betty had led rather disreputable lives. Their ship took fire in mid-ocean. They realized that the end was near and promised to reform if they were saved. What is most likely to happen? (TNFD, 3.9 P.E.)

(NM) The ship burned up and all on board were lost.

(M) A sudden cloudburst of rain put out the fire.

In both instances the movie children strain all probability to enable the "hero" to escape even when the only claim to being hero is having led a rather disreputable life.

11. *Special Dislikes*

As a catch-all for the purpose of following up clues suggested by the Character Education Inquiry, we presented in the first revision of the test a check list in which children were asked to check all the things they most disliked. In the second revision we divided this list into four shorter ones each containing six or seven items instructing the children to check in each list the three things most disliked. Only one of the twenty-six showed a significant difference in the proportion of checks from the two groups of children. Including the items of borderline significance, however, there are suggestive differences. The movie children checked the following more frequently as things most disliked: "having to help a slow child with his lessons," "laws restricting the liberty of the individual," "losing your best friend," while the non-movie children checked the following: "a famine in India," "having to read about a terrible famine in China," and "drinking parties." The center of concern for the movie child seems to be himself.

12. *Miscellaneous Differences*

The final revision of the tests included twenty-six questions testing a miscellaneous list of attitudes. Some of these had given probably significant differences but were difficult of any reasonable interpretation while others were included for the purpose of making certain that possible differences were not being prematurely discarded. This group yields only two clearly reliable differences. The movie children answer "true" to the statement "It is your duty to stick with your gang even when they go wrong" more often than non-movie children. This is one of the few questions taken directly from the Character Education Inquiry tests which has consistently elicited different responses from the two groups. All efforts to frame questions of the same type have failed to show a difference. A second question, also taken from the Character Education Inquiry tests, is as follows:

> Jim and the boys used to ride down the steep sidewalk very fast on their wagons and scooters and then turn the corner very sharply. What is most likely to happen? (TNFD, 8.3 P.E.)
>
> (NM)   It made other people uncomfortable seeing them do it.
>
> (M)   They tipped over and Jim was badly scratched up.

Apparently the element which differentiated the movie and non-movie children was the indifference of the movie and the concern of the non-movie children for others who are involved in the situation. Interestingly enough this item was retained for the purpose of making certain that there was no difference, since several items of the same type given to children in Troup Junior High failed to show differences.

Yet this unpromising question shows a difference more than eight times as large as its probable error—one of the largest which we have found.

Recreations and Attitudes toward Movies

We report here two additional types of data, one inferring attitudes and interests from recreations and one concerning attitudes toward the movies themselves. The basic data were obtained while giving the preliminary survey blank which was administered to all children (see Appendix C). Three hundred fifty-eight movie and 356 non-movie cases are involved.

Questions about recreations were intended primarily as exploratory devices from which attitudes might be inferred. It was hoped also that such data might answer the question whether very frequent movie-going tends to impoverish other recreational activities.

The children were asked to name the two things which they most commonly did for fun in the evening. Twenty-two per cent of the movie and 1 per cent of the non-movie name "going to the movies." Ten per cent of the movie and 4 per cent of the non-movie name social activities such as visiting, calling, parties, and lodge and club meetings. A larger proportion of the non-movie cases list "reading" and "playing games." These differences are reliable, varying from 4.3 to 12.8 times as large as their probable errors. A second question asked the children to list the things most commonly done for fun in the evening in which parents participated. Space was provided for naming six activities. The movie children named 2.9 and the non-movie 2.3 activities of this type. This difference is also highly reliable. In terms of quantity, there is no evidence of impoverishment in these data.

Two questions were asked about reading—the number of books read during the previous month and the names of the magazines which were read regularly. Again, there is no evidence of impoverishment as to amount of reading but rather the contrary. Fifty-eight per cent of the movie and 44 per cent of the non-movie report five or more books read the month prior to filling out the survey blank. Fifty-seven per cent of the movie and 40 per cent of the non-movie name two or more magazines. Both differences are reliable and in favor of the movie children.

Analysis of the magazines named, however, reveals qualitative differences from which attitudes and interests may be inferred. Four times as many movie as non-movie children (7.5 per cent and 1.7 per cent) mention "True Story" or "Love Story" or "Romance," etc. Twice as many movie as non-movie children name motion-picture magazines (20.9 per cent and 8.1 per cent), "Liberty" (11.4 per cent and 5.6 per cent), various adventure and western story magazines (11.4 per cent and 4.5 per cent), and aviation and air story magazines (9.2 per cent and 4.2 per cent). In contrast 17.3 per cent of the non-movie children and 11.6 per cent of the movie children name such magazines as "Scientific American" and "Popular Mechanics." All but two of these differences are reliable.

Another recreation from which interest is readily inferred is the number of dances. Twenty-eight per cent of the movie and 9 per cent of the non-movie children report one or more dances during the month prior to filling out the questionnaire.

It follows from the differences in movie habits that 70 per cent of the movie children and only 25 per cent of the non-movie children report that they are absent from home two or more evenings per week.

RESULTS OF THE ATTITUDES SURVEY

As a check on the composition of our two groups, the preliminary survey blank included several questions designed to get at attitudes toward the movies. A slightly larger proportion of the non-movie children when they do go to movies tend to go with some one and to go to shows which include vaudeville on their programs. As between movie and vaudeville, the movie children tend slightly to prefer the movie while non-movie children tend slightly to prefer the vaudeville.

"Would you go more often to movies if you had your own way?" Forty-three per cent of the movie children say "Yes" while only 21 per cent of the non-movie give this answer. The difference is ten times as large as would be apt to occur by chance. That is, we have not only large differences in habits of movie-going between our two groups but also large differences in their attitudes toward the movies themselves. Presumably the differences in attitudes are much larger than indicated, since 43 per cent of the movie children would like to go more often than three times a week while the 21 per cent of the non-movie children who would like to go more often are talking about going more often than a few times a year.

To the same effect are the reasons which movie and non-movie children give for their attendance. The question was framed as follows: "If you go to movies two or more times a week, why do you go so often? If you go to movies less than once a week, why don't you go more? Answer the question which applies to your case." Of considerable interest is the fact that 19 per cent of the movie children misinterpreted the question and instead of giving reasons for going so often gave reasons such as financial difficulties and parental disapproval for not going more often. Less than 1 per cent of the non-movie children made the reverse type of misinterpretation. Of the movie cases who properly answered the question 72 per cent replied that they liked movies and 28 per cent said that they had nothing else to do or went in order to pass the time. Of the non-movie children who answered the question, 56 per cent said they did not like movies, 14 per cent mentioned parental disapprovals, 12 per cent said they didn't have time or preferred some other activity, 12 per cent reported financial difficulties, and 6 per cent gave miscellaneous reasons.

The children were asked what type of movie they liked best. Twice as many non-movie (14.5 per cent) as movie (6.5 per cent) failed to answer the question. Mystery pictures were named by 33 per cent of the movie and 13 per cent of non-movie, the difference being more than eight times as large as its probable error. The movie children also name pictures of college life, dramatic pictures, pictures of romance, and crime pictures more frequently but the differences are not reliable. The non-movie children name comedy pictures more frequently than any other, 27 per cent expressing this preference in comparison with only 10 per cent of the movie cases. The difference is nearly eight times as large as its probable error. Non-movie children tend to name educational pictures, westerns, aviation, and sea pictures more frequently than movie children.

Summary of Findings

The center of interest of this chapter has been in the discovery of differences in the attitudes of movie and non-movie children. Throughout, pencil and paper test procedures have been used employing a wide variety of problems and questions. The evidence is that children give their own independent answers to such questions instead of trying to make a good showing and that their responses are fairly steady.

RESULTS OF THE ATTITUDES SURVEY 69

We began by comparing the responses of 102 children who go to movies three and four times a week with 101 children who go to movies once or twice a month to 774 individual test questions in the tests of moral knowledge, attitude, and opinion used by the Character Education Inquiry. A very wide variety of situations are involved, most of which carry distinctly ethical and moral implications. The findings are essentially negative.

Building on slender clues from this study and on observation of movies and suggestions of others we constructed an attitude test designed to verify twenty-nine specific hypotheses. This test was given to 106 movie and 102 non-movie cases in Troup Junior High. A revision directed at seventy-two specific hypotheses was given to 310 movie and 341 non-movie children in junior high schools of Norwalk, Connecticut, Fair Haven, Connecticut, and Dayton, Ohio. Combining, 416 movie and 443 non-movie cases have been studied intensively. On the average one group attends nearly three times a week while the other attends only a few times a year. The groups have been equated for age, school grade, intelligence, and socio-economic-educational home background. Having an equal proportion of boys and girls and equal proportions from each community makes the groups equal in these two respects. In addition, the children in Norwalk, Fair Haven, and Dayton have been equated for birthplace of parents.

The available evidence indicates that there are no differences in attitudes for or against athletes, prize fighters, sea captains, Mexicans, Japanese, Chinese, Arab chieftains, robbers, gang leaders, thieves, criminals, bootleggers, rum runners, or prohibition agents.

There are no distinguishable differences in approval of the enforcement of prohibition and in the stressing of the consequences of prohibition to individual convenience or to social welfare.

There is no evidence to show that the movie children believe that criminals reform and no evidence that movie children are militaristic.

Five approaches to sex attitudes show no differences or inconsistent and contradictory differences. There is no evidence to show that movie children believe in earlier marriage or that marriage is unsuccessful. Check lists of offenses and offenders which included disapproved sex attitudes showed no difference. Reasons for continuing or discontinuing to "date" with one of the opposite sex are inconsistent.

There is evidence to show that movie children admire or are more interested in cowboys, popular actors, dancers, and chorus girls while non-movie children are more interested in such types as the medical student and college professor. Interest in a type, however, does not indicate approval. In the case of chorus girls, the movie children more than non-movie children say that few chorus girls are worthwhile members of society. According to expectations the movie children tend to say that most policemen torture and mistreat those suspected of crime; that most Spaniards are impractical, romantic, and love-makers; that few Russians are kind and generous. Contrary to expectations, the movie children say that Protestant ministers are highly intelligent; the movie children deny that social workers are busybodies; the movie children believe that few Frenchmen are romantic and impractical.

While there is no evidence of approval or disapproval of prohibition, the movie children believe that there is much drinking and much violation of the prohibition laws.

While there are no differences in attitudes toward crime and criminals, there is some evidence that movie children believe that few criminals escape their just punishment. On the question of the criminal reforming and also involving indirectly sex attitudes, there is evidence showing that the movie children believe that feminine charms are more potent in reforming the criminal than fear of the police. There is evidence that under certain conditions the movie children expect the hero to carry the girl off by force or compel her to dance with him. No difference was found in approval or disapproval of such conduct. Akin to these two tendencies which involve judgment of what is likely to happen is the willingness of the movie children to strain all probability in order to enable the hero to escape.

Consistent with the data of Chapter II showing the movie children to be poorly adjusted to school is evidence showing that the movie children believe few teachers to be too easy and few schoolbooks to be interesting.

There is considerable evidence to show that movie children set special values on smart clothes and dressing well.

On the whole the evidence is that movie children are more sensitive to parental approvals and more discriminating in judging the things which they should get permission to do.

In the field of miscellaneous dislikes the movie children are relatively more indifferent to distress and famine in India and China and relatively more concerned over losing a good friend.

The movie children read more but the quality of their reading is not as high. They go to more dances. They report more recreations in which parents participate.

The movie children go to movies because they like them or have nothing else to do. Non-movie children do not go to movies because they dislike movies or have too much else to do. Parental disapprovals and financial difficulties are not more important in curtailing the attendance of non-movie than of movie children.

Two contrasts between these data and the findings from the Character Education Inquiry tests should be noted. The first and most striking is the high specificity of the attitude differences. Each difference stands on its own feet and seems unrelated to the others while the results of Chapter II present a reasonably integrated and consistent picture. Secondly, in the area of attitudes where we expected to find differences and labored diligently to frame questions to reveal them, the total of the findings is more negative than positive whereas the Character Education tests of conduct and ratings of reputation which seemed far removed from the movies have handsomely rewarded a modicum of labor with many significant differences.

CHAPTER V

OTHER DIFFERENCES BETWEEN MOVIE AND NON-MOVIE GROUPS

WE are postponing an interpretation of our findings until all the evidence for their evaluation is before the reader. Here we present further data and certain retabulations which are important in choosing between the several possible interpretations and in judging the significance of the motion-picture influence. Three questions will be considered. First, can the differences in conduct and attitude and in motion-picture attendance be explained on the ground of differences in the home backgrounds of the movie and non-movie children? Second, can the differences in conduct and attitude and in motion-picture attendance be explained on the ground that they are mutually reënforcing? Third, how important in comparison with other factors is the influence of the movies?

Parental Attitudes toward the Movies

Can the observed differences in conduct and attitude and in movie habits be explained as caused by some third factor? The most likely source for such a factor would be in the home backgrounds of our two groups of children. It is true that these groups are equated for socio-economic-educational background and for birthplace of parents. This equating, however, is far from insuring that the homes of the two groups are alike in all other respects. Indeed, it may be argued that the mere differences in movie habits of children is evidence that the parents of our two groups use radically different methods of control. If, as some of our friends have urged, the parents of movie children permit them to run wild while parents of non-movie children exercise careful and thorough supervision, this difference might well account both for the differences in movie attendance and for the differences in conduct and attitude.

We have already presented data which bear in directly on this question in connection with an attempt to determine whether there are differences between movie and non-movie children in their attitudes toward their parents. On the whole the evidence was that movie children are more sensitive to parental approvals and disapprovals and more discriminating in judging the things which they should get parental permission to do.

Evidence already presented indicates that the movie children go to movies because they like them or have nothing else to do while non-movie children do not go to movies because they dislike movies or have too much else to do. Parental disapprovals constitute only a minor factor in influencing the attendance of both movie and non-movie children.

More direct evidence on the question of parental supervision was sought through questions which were inserted in the preliminary survey blank and filled out by all children (see Appendix C). Three questions were asked: Do you usually go to the movies with your father or mother? Do your parents urge or discourage your going to the movies? What things do you do in the evening for fun in which your mother or father take part? From the Norwalk, Fair Haven, and Dayton populations we have tabulated the responses of 185 movie and 179 non-movie boys and of 173 movie and 167 non-movie girls.

Other Differences Between Groups

In answer to the first question the records supplied by the children show that 29 per cent of the movie and 35 per cent of the non-movie children say that they usually go to the movies with one or the other or both parents. The fact that non-movie children are more apt to go with their parents suggests greater care in the supervision of their movie-going, but the more probable explanation of this tendency is the fact that the parents of non-movie children themselves go to movies two or three times as often as their children. That is, when non-movie children go to the motion-picture theater they are more apt to go with their parents for the simple reason that their parents go two or three times as often. Conversely, the fact that only 29 per cent of the movie children say that they go with their parents is not an indication of poor supervision; rather it may be due to the fact that their parents go only a third as much.

In answer to the second question, 11 per cent of the movie and 5 per cent of the non-movie children say that their parents encourage movie-going. Fourteen per cent of the movie and 25 per cent of the non-movie children claim that their parents discourage movie attendance. Seventy-five per cent of the movie and 70 per cent of the non-movie children report that their parents neither encourage nor discourage movie attendance. These data indicate that both groups of parents are largely indifferent, with only a slightly greater concern on the part of the parents of the non-movie cases. It is to be noted, however, that the parents of the movie children are indifferent about two or more movies a week while the parents of the non-movie children are indifferent about one movie or less a month. We can only speculate as to the concern or the parents of the non-movie children should their children begin to go several times a week.

The third question asked the children to name the things which they most commonly did for fun in the evening and in which their parents participated. Space was provided for the listing of six activities. The movie children listed on the average 2.9 such activities while the non-movie children listed only 2.3. The difference is reliable, being 6.5 times as large as its probable error. The movie children naturally name "going to the movies" more frequently as an activity in which parents joint, but when these mentions are eliminated, they continue to name more such activities. There is no evidence here that movie children are turned loose to run wild.

These data are not wholly adequate to answer the question at issue, but their weight is in the direction of indifference for both groups of parents rather than in the direction of making one group indifferent and the other much concerned to the point of close supervision and prohibition of movie attendance.

Parental Habits of Motion-Picture Attendance

In the process of searching for differences in the home backgrounds of the movie and non-movie children which might explain the differences in conduct and attitude and in motion-picture attendance, we included in the preliminary survey blank questions concerning the frequency with which their mothers and fathers went to movies. The reliability of these reports was checked in two ways. First, the correlation between independent reports made by siblings are .624 for mothers and .591 for fathers. That is, a pair of siblings give similar reports for their parents. Second, the correlation between each child's statements of his own habits and those of his parents is .372 while the correlation of his own habits with his brother's or sister's

Other Differences Between Groups

reports of his parents' habits is .275. That is, children do not tend to impute to their parents habits similar to their own.

Comparing the motion-picture attendance habits of parents of movie and non-movie cases reveals large differences. On the average, the fathers of the movie children are said to go 3.4 times a month while fathers of non-movie children are said to go .9 times per month, a difference which is seventeen times as large as its probable error. Similar figures for mothers are 3.7 and 1.7 times per month, a difference which is twenty-three times as large as its probable error. These are by far the most extreme differences which we have found. Here, obviously, is a large difference in the home backgrounds of movie and non-movie children which may have a bearing on the differences in conduct and attitude and in movie attendance. Perhaps the distinguishing attitudes of movie children are aggravated by the fact that their parents are also frequent movie-goers.

For the purpose of studying the influence of the difference in parental movie habits we undertook to equate our movie and non-movie groups for frequency of parental attendance in addition to keeping them equated for sex, age, school grade, intelligence, socio-economic-educational backgrounds, nationality, and community. Differences in attitudes between the newly equated groups were then compared with differences found between the groups before the factor of parental habits was eliminated. Such comparisons were made using the responses to the five questions which had shown the largest differences between the movie and non-movie groups.

To the question "Which would you rather be, a college professor or a popular actor?" the original proportions of responses from the movie and non-movie groups in Norwalk, Fair Haven, and Dayton were as follows:

	College Professor	Popular Actor
281 Movie	45.6%	54.4%
268 Non-movie	70.1%	29.9%

Here the difference is 24.5 per cent. When the groups are equated for parental attendance, the difference falls to 21.4 per cent. Apparently there is some tendency for the differences in parental attendance to aggravate the contrast in the attitudes of movie and non-movie cases. As a check on this result, we compared the responses of movie children whose parents go frequently with the responses of movie children whose parents go infrequently. This comparison shows no difference. Comparing non-movie children whose parents go infrequently with non-movie children whose parents go frequently shows a difference of 16.8 per cent. Of non-movie children whose parents go infrequently, 77.9 per cent check "a college professor." This group shows a difference from all movie children of 32.3 per cent. Of non-movie children whose parents go frequently 61.1 per cent check "a college professor." This group shows a difference from all movie children of only 15.5 per cent.

Data for the other four questions which were studied are not consistent. Only one shows a very slight tendency for equating to decrease the difference, while three show a tendency for equating to increase the difference. That is, for three questions differences in parental attendance obscure rather than exaggerate the differences in attitudes. The evidence from all five questions, accordingly, is that parental attendance is not a determining factor in the differences in attitudes which we have reported.

OTHER DIFFERENCES BETWEEN GROUPS

The Relation of Age and Experience to the Differences between Movie and Non-Movie Groups

Besides the additional light thrown on the problem by the data on parental attitudes we have still further data which are valuable as aids in the interpretation of our results. One such datum is the relation of age to differences between movie and non-movie groups. Another is the correlation between frequency of attendance and such factors as deportment, school marks, and character tests.

To test the relation between age level and differences in conduct and attitudes we divided our cases into three groups: those under eleven and a half years old, those eleven and a half years old and under thirteen, and those thirteen years and older. The youngest group contained 35 movie and 33 non-movie cases, the middle group 39 movie and 39 non-movie, and the oldest 28 movie and 29 non-movie cases. We tabulated the scores of these three pairs of groups on the following Character Education Inquiry tests: total reputation, scholastic marks, deportment, guess who, total coöperation, efficiency coöperation, pictures coöperation, and school honesty. With the two exceptions of deportment and school honesty the differences between movie and non-movie cases become progressively larger with advancing age. The younger non-movie children stand on the average .26 sigma deviations above the younger movie children; the middle group of non-movie children stand .47 sigma deviations above the middle group of movie children; and the older non-movie children stand on the average .53 sigma deviations above the older movie children. That is, the difference between movie and non-movie children eleven and a half years old or older is about twice as great as the difference between movie and non-movie children under eleven and a half years old.

For the purpose of answering the question: "Does more and more movie attendance mean progressively lower and lower scores?" we plotted the total reputation, deportment, and total coöperation scores against frequency of movie attendance using all cases. The tabulations were made separately for grades five to six and grades seven and eight, and separately by sex and population. Translating the average scores for each level of movie attendance into sigma deviations and averaging the results of the several tabulations we have the following: Those who go less than once a week stand .23 sigma deviations above the average of all cases, those who go once a week stand .04 sigma deviations below the average of all cases, those who go three times a week stand .31 sigma deviations below the average of all cases, and those who go four or more times a week (an average of 4.5 times) stand .48 sigma deviations below the average of all cases. That is, each added increment of motion-picture attendance results in a series of equally lower and lower scores.

These data tend to give some support to the interpretation that children who have the conduct tendencies and attitudes of the typical movie-goer are attracted to the movies and that movie-going stimulates and reënforces the very tendencies which originally attract children to the movies. We shall return to this question in the last chapter.

The Relative Strength of Movie Influence as Compared with Other Influences in Determining Attitudes

From the data thus far presented it is apparent that the movies are *only one* of a larger number of forces which determine the attitudes and conduct of school children. That the movies are an influence there is no doubt. The question concerns the degree and kind of influence which

OTHER DIFFERENCES BETWEEN GROUPS

they exert and on what types of children. We present here certain data having a direct bearing on this point.

In the first place it will be recalled that the largest differences which we found between movie and non-movie groups were in (a) reputation as measured by the Character Education Inquiry Tests, (b) school deportment, and (c) measures of coöperation behavior. When all children on whom we had data, including movie, non-movie and all others in between, are considered, the coefficients of correlation between frequency of movie attendance and these three factors are very low. They are −.156 for reputation, −.273 for deportment, and −.186 for coöperation. Corrected for errors of measurement they become −.252, −.441, and −.311. These low correlations can mean only one thing and that is that movie attendance is only slightly or moderately related to reputation, deportment, and coöperation. Correlation, of course, does not mean causation, but even if it did one would have to say that in this case the movies are not a very significant causal factor. Furthermore the Character Education Inquiry reports sixteen coefficients of correlation between reputation and other factors (not including the movies) and every one of these except one is larger than the coefficient reputed above between movie attendance and reputation.[1] The Character Education Inquiry also reports a correlation (corrected for attenuation) of .943 between reputation and a pool of 37 conduct tests. All of this points to the conclusion that the low reputation of the movie group is not due to frequenting the movies but rather that frequency of movie attendance is one of the things which children of low reputation ratings do.

Another interesting side light is the fact that when *all* the children of one community are compared with all of

[1] Hartshorne and May, *Studies in the Organization of Character*, p. 234.

another community, the difference between them in attitudes is much greater than between movie and non-movie children of the same community. A systematic study of each test element shows a total of 59 which yield larger differences between children in different communities than the largest difference found between movie and non-movie cases. Some of these differences are exceptionally large. For example, 55 per cent of the Fair Haven and only 7 per cent of the Dayton cases respond "No" to the statement "All Most Many Some Few No school rules should be changed." Fifty-eight per cent of the Fair Haven and only 17 per cent of the Dayton children respond "All" to the statement "All Most Many Some Few No crooks could make a living honestly if they wanted to." When given the following choice "Which would you rather do in a baseball game, hit a home run or help make a double play?" 76 per cent of the children in Troup Junior High and only 36 per cent of the Dayton children elect to make a home run.

In Chapter IV evidence was presented showing that the community may be important in influencing the difference between movie and non-movie cases. In answer to the question, "Which would you rather be, a college professor or a popular actor?", the Troup and Norwalk movie and non-movie cases differed by only 11 per cent while in Dayton the difference was 50 per cent.

Summary

The method of selecting children for study and the additional data of this chapter indicate rather clearly that differences in home backgrounds cannot account for either the differences in movie habits or the differences in conduct and attitude. The original selection of movie and non-movie children was made in such a way that the two groups are alike as to the educational, economic, and cultural status of their homes. The data of this chapter suggest that the parents of the two groups are also alike in their indifference to the movie habits of their children and in their supervision of their children's other activities. At only one point are the parents of the movie and non-movie children dissimilar, *i.e.*, the parents of movie children are said to go to movies more often than parents of non-movie children. The evidence, however, is that this difference obscures as much as it increases the differences in attitudes.

Each added increment of frequency of motion-picture attendance is accompanied by progressively lower scores on the three most significant tests of the Character Education Inquiry. The differences between movie and non-movie children increase with age. If anything these results favor the theory that differences in movie habits, conduct, and attitude are mutually reënforcing as opposed to the theory that one set of differences is the cause of the other.

Factors of age, intelligence, school grade, and home background are as important and possibly more important in influencing the conduct and attitudes of children as the movie. In the case of attitudes, the influence of the community far overshadows in importance the influence of the movie.

CHAPTER VI

SUMMARY AND INTERPRETATIONS

Two groups of school children in grades 5 to 9, one attending the movies two or more times a week and the other attending the movies once a month or less, were equated in respect to sex, age, intelligence, school grade, home background, nationality, and community, and were compared in respect to a wide variety of measures of attitude and conduct. Significant differences between the groups were found in ratings for reputation by teachers and classmates, in school grades, in deportment, in tests of coöperation, and in a number of attitude patterns which are found in the movies. No significant differences were found in the conduct tests of persistence, self-control, and honesty in out of school situations; nor in measures of moral knowledge, and social attitudes on a wide variety of topics most of which were unrelated to the movies; nor on a great many types of attitudes which are definitely related to the movies.[1] On the whole the data tend to favor the non-movie group.

Of the total number of comparisons made between the movie and non-movie groups including conduct tests, school grades and deportment, attitude tests and questionnaire, significant differences favoring the non-movie group appeared in about 8 per cent of the comparisons, favoring the movie groups in about 2 per cent, and favoring neither (*i.e.*, no difference) in about 90 per cent.[2]

---
[1] See summaries at the end of Chapters II to V.
[2] These proportions are only the roughest approximations.

Concerning the 90 per cent of the comparisons which showed no significant differences we may say (1) that the movies are exerting no influence in these areas, or (2) that differences in these areas are not such as would cause differences in movie habits, or (3) that other factors such as community differences tend to obscure real differences, or (4) that one type of movie is exerting strong influence in one direction which is canceled by an opposite influence from another movie. For example, the Chinese are shown favorably in "Son of the Gods" and unfavorably in "Welcome Danger."

Concerning the 10 per cent of comparisons which showed significant differences we may say (1) that these differences are caused directly by the movies, or (2) that the movies exert a selective rather than a causal influence and that these differences are causes of attendance rather than results, or (3) that the equating process was not observed far enough and the differences were thus due in part to other unknown causes, or (4) that movie habits and these attitudes are interacting forces.

For convenience of discussion we shall label these four interpretations as movie influence theories, selection theories, third factor theories, and interaction theories. Each will be discussed briefly in turn.

I. *Movie Influence Theories*

It cannot be denied on the whole, and especially concerning the tests of the Character Education Inquiry, that the movie children make a poorer showing than the non-movie children. The critics of the movies will find themselves drawn strongly to any explanation which places the responsibility for the poorer showing of the frequent attenders at the door of the motion-picture theater. The argument that the observed differences are caused by differences in exposure to movies takes two forms.

(1) *The Specific Influence Theory* asserts that the movies portray a large number of specific conduct patterns and character types which with constant repetition finally carry over into conduct and attitude. According to this theory, the test of whether a difference is to be attributed to the movies' influence depends upon whether a corresponding pattern can be found on the motion-picture screen. A large portion of the questions in the attitudes tests were devised on this theory. We observed movies and obtained the judgment of other observers for the purpose of discovering such patterns. Appendix B presents a rather complete blue print of the patterns which we or others believed were portrayed on the motion-picture screen. A large proportion of the differences which turned out according to this list of hypotheses may be attributed to the influence of the motion picture. Differences of this type are as follows: The movie children tend to say that most policemen torture and mistreat those suspected of crime; that most Spaniards are impractical, romantic, and love-makers; that few Russians are kind and generous; that there is much drinking and violation of prohibition laws; and that few criminals escape their just punishment. The merit of this explanation of such differences is strengthened by a further negative test; that is, it requires an extraordinary stretch of imagination to explain such differences on the ground that children with these attitudes would tend to seek the movies.

The Specific Influence Theory is on somewhat less solid ground when it attributes to the movie influence such differences as the following: The movie children tend to admire or be more interested in cowboys, popular actors, dancers, chorus girls, and less interested in such types as the medical student and the college professor; the movie children tend to strain all probability in order to enable the hero to escape; the movie children are more interested in clothes and dressing well; the movie children go to more dances and read movie magazines, "True Story," and "Love Story" more frequently. These differences meet the first test; that is, similar attitude patterns are portrayed on the motion-picture screen but they do not fully meet the second or negative test. Possibly children with these attitudes and interests would be the very ones attracted to the movie theater.

Keeping in mind the limitations suggested by the word "possibly," the authors are in sympathy with this theory as here formulated. It is fortified by the fact that it claims only such differences as were claimed prior to the establishing of the differences. Its chief merit is that it does not attempt to explain all of the differences.

(2) *The General Influence Theory* would go much further. It asserts that the general tone and atmosphere of the average movie is at least undesirable if not pernicious in ways which are difficult to specify precisely and that constant exposure to this atmosphere is responsible for the poor showing of the movie children. This theory would place all the differences in coöperation, reputation, scholastic standing, and deportment which appear from the analysis of the Character Education Inquiry material at the door of the motion-picture theater.

The authors are not inclined to agree with this theory, while not denying that it may contain elements of truth. Its chief difficulty is that it assumes a poorer performance in general by the movie children. It would require a poorer showing on the persistence and inhibition tests as well as on the coöperative ones. It would require the movie children to be more dishonest out of school as well as in school. It would make the ethical perceptions of the movie children less keen instead of equally keen. While on the whole the movie children fail to compare favorably with the non-movie children, the evidence is that their failures are specific rather than general.

II. *Selection Theories*

The selection theories are of various kinds, but all have the common element of asserting that some of the differences are just such as would attract certain children to the movies and cause others to dislike the movies. The most concise and concrete way of stating these theories is to outline the experiment which they would suggest. First, select several communities which do not have and have not had a motion-picture theater. Second, select from these communities all children of low deportment and scholastic standing, of poor reputation, who are uncoöperative, who are interested in cheap reading, who most admire cowboys, dancers, actors, and so on. Third, introduce a motion-picture theater into these communities and observe the children who develop habits of frequent movie attendance. The selection theories assert that the selected group of children will be found to be going more frequently than other children. In more detailed form, these theories may be formulated as follows:

(1) *The Docility Theory* asserts that the non-movie children are docile and conforming, while the movie children are simply normal children full of life and energy who have run afoul of the hard mechanism of the school. This theory points to the fact that the non-movie children do not go to movies as evidence of such conformity—in this case conformity to parental prohibitions against movie going. According to this theory the low deportment of the movie

children is a sign of independence and self-reliance. It cites studies such as that of Wickham showing that teachers generally tend to penalize such innocuous behavior as "whispering," "tardiness," "impertinence," etc. The judgment of the authors is quite against this theory. It accounts for only a few of the facts and does not account very well for these. As for mere non-attendance at movies being indicative of conformity to parental approvals and disapprovals, data presented in the previous chapter indicates that there is no evidence of differences in parental efforts to control children's activities. While high deportment might have been indicative of docility and conformity in the schools of two or three generations ago, to-day high deportment plus scholastic achievement beyond what would be expected from intelligence can mean only lively interest in school work. It is true that teachers penalize certain behaviors which interfere with the orderly running of the schoolroom more than is warranted by their importance for the development of personality. The facts remain, however, that teachers' ratings are supported by the judgments of children, which are not biased by the necessity of keeping order. Moreover, this theory fails to account for the fact that teacher and pupil ratings as to coöperation show differences, while ratings as to honesty do not.

(2) *The Selection by Interests Theory* is more satisfactory. This theory begins by assuming two groups of children with different interests. One group cares little about school work and is more interested in a thrill, in fine clothes, in dancing, etc. The theory points to the differences in scholastic standing and school adjustment and to differences in interests as supporting the existence of such a group and asserts that this group would naturally gravitate to the movies. A second group is interested in school work, practical and serious

minded, and so busy with these interests that the movies hold no appeal.

(3) A third variation is the *Maladjustment Theory* which attempts to account for the differences revealed by the Character Education Inquiry data. Instead of viewing the many differences which we have found as so many separate findings, it asserts that the best interpretation is to regard all of them as symptoms of maladjustment on the part of the movie children—especially maladjustment in relation to school and to others. It asserts that the maladjusted child seeks the movies as an avenue of escape from unpleasant and irritating situations. According to this theory the difference between movie and non-movie children in reputation, coöperation, etc., are causes of rather than results of the differences in movie habits. This theory readily accounts for the disadvantage of the movie children in deportment, scholastic marks, teacher ratings, and pupil ratings. Such maladjustment would be more apt to appear on tests of coöperation than on tests of persistence and self-control. The theory would account for the cheating of the movie group in school situations and the absence of differences in honesty as tested in out-of-school situations.

(4) *The Non-Participation Theory* centers its attention on the relation between two facts. It points out that non-participation is one of the essential features of movie going. For two or three hours, three or four times a week, the movie children are spectators, passive and being entertained. They may identify themselves with the hero just as the football crowd cheers for one team or the other, but they take no active part. This theory would point out the striking fact that when the separate elements of ratings and conduct tests are considered, the largest differences appear in the area of coöperation. When children are given the chance

of participating in a common enterprise to win a prize for the class, the movie children fail to do their share and work harder for the individual prize. This theory would claim that children with the spectator and non-participating habit would tend to prefer the movie as an avenue of recreation. While this theory does not account for all the differences, it is most suggestive as far as it goes. According to this theory excessive movie attendance should be discouraged even if the things portrayed on the motion-picture screen were quite above reproach.

The several selection theories contain substantial elements of truth and within limits provide plausible explanations of many of the differences which have been reported. The chief difficulty with these theories is that they leave no room for the movie influence to aid and abet the original differences which are assumed.

III. *Third Factor Theories*

The essence of Third Factor Theories is that they attempt to trace both the differences in movie habits and in character and attitude to some other factor. In Chapter V we presented considerable data on two variations of this view. Our conclusion was that differences in extent of parental control and differences in amount of parental movie going could not be used to explain both the differences in attendance and in conduct and attitude.

An intriguing and suggestive interpretation of this type is the *Sleep Disturbance Theory*. It relies on data collected by Dr. Renshaw on the influence of movie attendance on children's sleep. Dr. Renshaw measured the amount of sleeplessness as evidenced by movements of the child's bed recorded by ingenious apparatus. Comparing the sleep on movie nights with that on normal or non-movie nights, he found that children had more difficulty in going to sleep and slept less well following a movie. These data at once suggest a causal sequence: attendance at a movie, disturbed sleep, irritability the next morning, maladjustment.

IV. *The Interaction Theory*

The Interaction Theory is concerned for the most part to place limits upon an extreme formulation of the selection type of explanation. While admitting the force of the suggestion that children with certain interests would naturally gravitate to the movies, this theory would add that the movies probably stimulate these interests. While the maladjusted child may seek to escape from his difficulties by going to the movies, this theory would point out that motion-picture attendance contains no promise of relieving the source of the difficulty. While the non-participating and uncoöperative child may get more satisfaction out of being entertained by the movies than out of providing his own entertainment, the Interaction Theory asserts that continued movie going probably aggravates the spectator habit. While this theory admits the suggestiveness of the sequence, "attendance at a movie, disturbed sleep, irritability, maladjustment," it would amend the sequence by adding "more movie attendance." According to this view, the rôle of the movie is not a primary one. It does not create special interests or maladjustment or the spectator habit. Rather it aids or abets or increases or aggravates differences between children which were already operating to cause some to seek and others to avoid the motion-picture theater.

The facts revealed by this study seem best to fit the Specific Influence Theory and the Interaction Theory. That the movies exert an influence there can be no doubt. But it is our opinion that this influence is specific for a given

Summary and Interpretations

child and a given movie. The same picture may influence different children in distinctly opposite directions. Thus in a general survey such as we have made, the net effect appears small. We are also convinced that among the most frequent attendants the movies are drawing children who are in some way maladjusted and whose difficulties are relieved only in the most temporary manner and are, in fact, much aggravated. In other words, the movies tend to fix and further establish the behavior patterns and types of attitudes which already exist among those who attend most frequently.

APPENDIX A

THE VALIDITY OF CHILDREN'S REPORTS OF THEIR MOVIE HABITS

THE general procedure of this study has been to compare children who go to the movies very frequently with children who go infrequently. We have found it convenient to base our selection on the statements of the children themselves. Two standards for determining the trustworthiness of these reports have been employed, (a) that of internal consistency, and (b) that of agreement with independent criteria.

Consistency of Several Reports

For the purpose of testing the internal consistency of children's own statements of their movie habits we have available four sets of data. Among the 850 children in grades five to eight who were studied intensively by the Character Education Inquiry, 419 made two reports of their movie habits. One report was in response to the question, "How many times a week do you go to the movies?" The other was taken from detailed time schedules of activities which children filled out Monday of one week, Tuesday of the next week, and so on for seven weeks. Comparing these two reports gives a correlation of .44.

Secondly, we have the answers of 1261 children in Troup Junior High of New Haven, Conn., to the following questions submitted to them in May, 1929.

1. How often have you gone to the movies (not counting movies during school hours) in the past year? Check on the dotted line *after* the most correct answer. Never been......; Been only a few times ....; Go once a month......; Go twice a month......; Go three times a month......; Once a week......; Twice a week....; Three times a week......; Four times a week......; Five times a week......; Six times a week.......

2. How often have you gone to movies since Christmas vacation?.......
3. About how many times have you gone to movies (other than movies during school hours) during the past month?.......

The intercorrelations of the answers to these questions are .70, .60, and .67.

Thirdly, we have the answers of 677 children in grades eight and nine of Troup Junior High to a similar set of three questions submitted to them in November, 1929. As in the earlier set, the first question covered the previous year, while the second and third asked about their movie habits during the summer and fall. The intercorrelations of the answers to these three questions are .50, .60, and .47.

Fourthly, we may compare the statements of these 677 children made in November with their statements made six months earlier in May. Combining the answers to each set of questions and correlating gives a coefficient of .59.

Our judgment is that the last of these values is a close approximation to the minimum reliability of a composite score combining the answers to three questions such as the set quoted above. Possibly .59 is too high due to spurious memory factors; more probably it is too low due to actual changes in movie habits.

Agreement with Independent Criteria

The trustworthiness of children's reports of their movie habits has been checked against two independent criteria: statements of their mothers and statements of their siblings. The questionnaires submitted to 677 children in Troup Junior High during November, 1929, asked for street addresses. Two weeks later a letter was sent to 200 homes of these children explaining that a "movie census" was being taken and requesting their coöperation. Two census-takers called at these homes and obtained the mothers' reports as to the movie habits of 123 children. We avoided the appearance of checking the truthfulness of the child's own statement by collecting data about the motion-picture habits of all members of the family. Collusion between the child and mother was avoided by mailing a few letters each evening and visiting the homes the next day before the child's return from school. If a mother were not at home, a return call was not attempted. The mothers interviewed were all those of certain streets selected on the basis of accessibility. Their coöperation was excellent, only five refusing the information desired. The question was first addressed to the mother herself and then concerning each member of the family in the following form: "On the average, how often have you gone to movies during the past year?" Comparing the oral statements of mothers with their children's statements made in May and November yields correlations of .35 and .43. Assuming that the oral statements of mothers are as reliable as their children's (.59), then the coefficient of .43 corrected for attenuation becomes .73.

Siblings of approximately the same age and in the same or adjacent school grades should have similar movie habits. Among the 1176 children in three Junior High Schools of Norwalk, Conn., we found 125 pairs of siblings. All were in grades seven, eight, or nine, and the average difference in their ages was only 1.53 years. The report of one sibling concerning his own movie habits when correlated with the report of another sibling concerning his own movie habits gives a coefficient of .60. It is obvious that the reliability of such reports must be at least .60. If the true correlation between the movie habits of a pair of siblings is assumed to be .90, then the usual formula may be rearranged to determine the reliability which applied to the obtained value of .60 will yield .90. This procedure indicates that the reliability of children's reports is .67.

Summary

Children's reports of their movie habits are far from perfectly consistent or perfectly in agreement with other reports. Errors of memory, carelessness, and probably changing habits are reflected in their statements. The similar data from internal evidence and from independent criteria, however, indicate that children's reports are relatively free from constant errors and from deliberate misrepresentation. The reliability of their reports is at least .60 and possibly .70. Such reports should correlate .78 or .84 with theoretically perfect measures. For the purpose of selecting the most frequent and the most infrequent movie goers and for the purpose of comparing large numbers of cases, the reports of children are entirely adequate.

APPENDIX B

CATALOGUE OF HYPOTHESES WHICH WERE VERIFIED, NOT VERIFIED, OR REVERSED

PRELIMINARY to the preparation of the attitudes test in its final form a very complete statement of the hypotheses involved was prepared. The following pages present the list of hypotheses as formulated prior to the testing together with the number of test questions directed toward each. With the results of the testing available, we may readily test each hypothesis for verification, reversal, or failure of verification. The statement follows exactly the original formulation save that we have inserted the words Verified, Partially Verified, Not Verified, and Reversed. Counting these labels, our batting average is as follows: Verified 18, Partially Verified 22, Not Verified 28, and Reversed 3. However, 17 of the 22 partial verifications are rather colorless, since the hypothesis is sometimes stated merely that there is a difference without specifying its nature. Of the 18 verifications, 5 are for hypotheses stating the tendency to be the opposite of expectations from critics of the movies. "Not Verified" of course does not mean that there *is* no difference, but simply that we have failed to find it in sufficiently clear form to warrant the statement that it is probably significant.

REVISED HYPOTHESES—MOTION-PICTURE STUDY

HYPOTHESIS a: HEROES AND BOOBS OF THE MOVIES

Statement of: That movie and non-movie children express different attitudes toward cowboys, college professors, chorus girls, dancers, prohibition agents, athletes, prize fighters, sea captains, policemen, social workers, etc., etc. That supplementary data will trace these differential attitudes to things seen on the motion-picture screen. *Partially Verified.*

Notes: Hypothesis d concerning criminals contains items which may be regarded as a special instance of the above. Note also that prohibition agents and supporters are included here and not under hypothesis c.

Number and distribution of items: Original test contained 26 items of which 16 have been retained. Twenty-five new items have been devised, making a total of 41. Most of the items are of the All-Most-Many-Some-Few-No type. Four true-false statements are taken from the four items which showed the largest difference on the All-Most-Many-Some-Few-No type of question.

Specific formulations

aa The movie children tend to say that college professors are sickly, weak, impractical men who have to wear glasses. *Partially Verified.* — 4 items

ab The movie children tend to say that small town police and detectives are inefficient and lacking in intelligence. *Not Verified.* — 3 items

ac The movie children tend to say that few supporters of prohibition are sincere and just. *Verified.* — 4 items

ad* The movie children tend to deny the charge that prohibition agents are fanatics and extremists. *Not Verified.* — 2 items

ae The movie children tend to admire prize fighters and athletes. *Not Verified.* — 5 items

af* The movie children tend to have a low regard for chorus girls. *Verified.* — 3 items

ag The movie children tend to admire professional dancers. *Verified.* — 2 items

ah* The movie children do not admire sea captains as much as non-movie children do. *Not Verified.* — 2 items

ai The movie children tend to say that social reformers are meddlers, busybodies, insincere, and inefficient. *Reversed.* — 3 items

aj* The movie children deny the charge that policemen are rough and bullying. *Partially Verified.* — 4 items

ak* The movie children tend to say that Protestant ministers are above average intelligence. *Verified.* — 2 items

al The movie children tend to admire cowboys. *Verified.* — 3 items

am Miscellaneous. — 4 items

Hypothesis b: National Groups

Statement of: The movie children have different attitudes from non-movie children toward Mexicans, Chinese, Spaniards, Arabs, Russians, Japanese, Italians, and Frenchmen. *Partially Verified.*

* In these five instances the available data indicate attitudes on the part of movie children just the opposite of what has been charged by critics of the movies.

Number and distribution of items: The original test contained 16 items of which 13 have been retained. Twenty-one new items have been devised, making a total of 34. Twenty-nine of these are of the All-Most-Many-Some-Few-No type. The five true-false items are restatements of the five most significant items.

Specific formulations

- *ba* The movie children tend to say that Mexicans are half-breeds, dirty, bandits, dishonest, and uncivilized. *Not Verified.* — 5 items
- *bb* The movie children tend to say that Chinese are cunning, underhand, the tools of criminal gangs, and easily excited to tong warfare. *Not Verified.* — 5 items
- *bc* The movie children tend to say that few Spaniards are desirable citizens for the United States and that most Spaniards are romantic and impractical. *Partially Verified.* — 3 items
- *bd** The movie children deny that most Arab chieftains are handsome men and fierce fighters. *Verified.* — 3 items
- *be* The movie children tend to say that Arabs in general are cruel, greedy, and terrible fighters. *Not Verified.* — 2 items
- *bf* The movie children tend to say that few Russians are kind, generous, or desirable citizens for the United States. *Verified.* — 4 items
- *bg* The movie children tend to say that Japanese are not desirable citizens for the United States. *Not Verified.* — 5 items
- *bh** The movie children tend to approve of most Italians as citizens of the United States. *Not Verified.* — 4 items
- *bi* The movie children tend to say that Frenchmen are ladies' men, love-makers, and impractical. *Reversed.* — 3 items

Hypothesis c: Prohibition

Statement of: There are differences in the attitudes of movie and non-movie children toward (1) the need for enforcement of prohibition, (2) the relative importance of the social *versus* individual consequences of prohibition, (3) benefits of prohibition, and especially (4) toward the prevalence of drinking and violation of the law. *Partially Verified.*

Notes: Hypotheses *ac* and *ad* are to be distinguished from the above formulation. Hypothesis *cc* below might be grouped under *cb*. Contrast *ch* below with *ac*.

Number and distribution of items: The original test contained 35 items under four hypotheses as directed above. The first three failed to

* Attitudes contrary to suggestions made by critics of the movies.

show clear trends. Of 21 items originally under these three hypotheses, only seven are retained and only four added. The fourth aspect of the above hypothesis concerning prevalence of drinking originally contained 14 items, of which 11 are retained and eight added. A wide variety of test procedures is employed.

Specific formulations

- *ca* There are differences in attitudes toward the need for stricter enforcement of prohibition laws. (Note direction of difference is not specified; the available data indicate movie boys contradicting tendency of movie girls.) *Not Verified.* — 2 items
- *cb* The movie children tend to say that drinking is of consequence only to the individual. *Not Verified.* — 3 items
- *cc* The movie children tend to say that the social consequences of enforcement or of license are less important than consequences to rights and interests of individuals. *Not Verified.* — 4 items
- *cd* The movie children tend to deny the charge that drinking by respectable and prominent persons is harmful. *Not Verified.* — 2 items
- *ce* The movie children tend to say that liquor is easily obtainable anywhere to those who want it. *Not Verified.* — 4 items
- *cf* The movie children tend to say that football games, dances, and parties are occasions for much drinking. *Verified.* — 7 items
- *cg* The movie children tend to say that few adult men have abstained from drinking since the passage of the prohibition amendment. *Verified.* — 3 items
- *ch** The movie children deny the current allegation that the politically dry are in practice wet. *Verified.* — 2 items
- *ci* Miscellaneous: the practice of college men, doctors, laborers, farmers. *Not Verified.* — 4 items

Hypothesis *d:* Criminals

Statement of: There are differences in the attitudes of movie and nonmovie children in their attitudes (1) toward the intelligence, bravery, and virtues of the criminal, (2) toward the certainty with which justice is done to the criminal offender, and (3) toward the likelihood of reform of criminals. *Partially Verified.*

Notes: Distinguish *df* from *eg.*

* Attitudes contrary to suggestions made by critics of the movies.

APPENDIX B 103

Number and distribution of items: The original test contained 14 items, mostly of the All-Most-Many-Some-Few-No type. Twelve are retained and 15 added.

Specific formulations:
- da The movie children tend to say that most or many criminals, thieves, hold-up men, etc., are brave, courageous, nervy. *Not Verified.* — 6 items
- db The movie children tend to say that many criminals have good qualities, are honorable in their way, etc. *Not Verified* — 4 items
- dc The movie children tend to say that many criminals are clever, intelligent, and could make a living honestly if they wished. *Not Verified.* — 6 items
- de* The movie children tend to believe that criminals finally are brought to justice and punished. *Verified.* — 4 items
- df* The movie children tend to believe that few criminals reform and turn out to be decent citizens. *Not Verified.* — 5 items
- dg* The movie children tend to deny the statement that gang leaders are good-looking, generous, etc. *Verified.* — 2 items

HYPOTHESIS e: SEX

Statement of: There are differences in the attitudes of movie and non-movie children toward marriage, rudeness to women, influence of women, desirable conduct with opposite sex, etc., etc. *Partially Verified.*

The Problem: A direct study of attitudes toward relations between the sexes, marriage, and related questions is out of the question in the public schools. The importance of the problem has led to the attempt to sample these attitudes in indirect ways.

Notes: Distinguish eb from ec. Distinguish eg from df.

Number and distribution of items: The original test contained a check list of 28 items and 15 other items. Of these only eight in their original form. The check list has been completely revised in order to escape a generalized type of response. The revised test contains 22 items employing many forms.

Specific formulations
- ea Movie children tend to believe in early marriage. *Not Verified.* — 2 items
- eb The movie children tend to believe that marriage is unsuccessful. *Not Verified.* — 3 items
- ec The movie children tend to believe that successful marriage is dependent on financial income. *Not Verified* — 4 items

* Attitudes contrary to suggestions made by critics of the movies.

ed	In a check list of offenses the movie children tend to check "telling smutty stories," etc., less frequently than non-movie children. *Not Verified.*	1 item
ee	In descriptions of disliked pupils the movie children tend to check "Boy crazy," etc., less frequently than non-movie children. *Not Verified.*	4 items
ef	In lists of reasons for discontinuing or continuing to "date" with one of the opposite sex, the movie children tend to check different reasons than non-movie children. *Partially Verified.*	4 items
eg	The movie children tend to believe that women exert a strong influence in helping criminal reform. *Verified.*	2 items
eh	The movie children tend to expect and justify assaults or rudeness to women. *Verified.*	2 items

Hypothesis *f*: School

Statement of: There are differences in the attitudes of movie and non-movie children toward school, teachers, schoolmates, schoolbooks, etc. *Partially Verified.*

Number and distribution of items: The original test contained 16 items. Eleven were retained and one added. The All-Most-Many-Some-Few-No test method is used exclusively.

No specific formulations: The retained items show many clear differences but the contradictions are too many and various to permit of formulation.

Hypothesis *g*: Clothes

Statement of: There are differences in the attitudes of movie and non-movie children toward clothing and the rôle of clothing in making for popularity. *Verified.*

Notes: Note that *ga* and *gb* contain implicit contradictions.

Number and distribution of items: The original test contained 9 items, 4 of which are retained and 7 added.

Specific formulations

ga	The movie children tend to say that good clothes add to the attractiveness of a girl. *Verified.*	3 items
gb	The movie children tend to deny the idea that popularity is a matter of good clothes. *Reversed.*	3 items
gc	The movie children tend to say that good clothes are essential to parties and dances. *Verified.*	3 items
gd	Miscellaneous.	2 items

Hypothesis *h:* Militarism

Statement of: There are differences in the attitudes of movie and non-movie children toward war, the benefits of war, etc. *Not Verified.*
Number and distribution of items: The original test contained eight items only, three of which are retained. Seven items are added. The additions are mostly of the All-Most-Many-Some-Few-No type, whereas the original test included only true-false.
No specific formulations.

Hypothesis *i:* Parents

Statement of: There are differences in the attitudes of movie and non-movie children toward the home and parents. *Partially Verified.*
Number and distribution of items: The original tests contained 31 items made up of 7 true-false statements, 4 multiple choices, and a check list of 20 items, asking when parental permission should be obtained. Only the check list of 20 items is retained, and to this is added 13 items. Two new test procedures are included containing a total of 23 items. The total of items is 56.

ia The movie children more frequently than the non-movie children say that one should get parental permission "to smoke," "to stay out after nine o'clock," etc. *Not Verified.*   33 items

ib In a list of sources of disagreement with parents the movie children check different items than non-movie children. *Partially Verified.*   11 items

ic In a list of traits desirable in a father or mother the movie children check different items than non-movie children. *Partially Verified.*   12 items

Hypothesis *j:* Escape from Danger

Statement of: The movie children tend to believe in the probability of the hero's escape from threatening danger. *Verified.*
Number and distribution of items: The original test contained 3 items all of which are retained and none added.
No specific formulations.

APPENDIX C

A SURVEY OF CERTAIN LEISURE TIME HABITS

These questions are for the purpose of finding out what you do during your leisure time. Answer the questions as completely and accurately as possible.

1. Your name .... Age ....
   Last name first
2. Boy or girl? .... School grade ....
3. Name of school .... Home-room teacher ....
4. What is your father's occupation? ....
5. Do your parents own an auto other than a truck? ......
6. Do you have a Victrola or Edison or Radio in your home? ......
7. How many daily papers do you take in your home? ....
8. Do you have a telephone in your home? ......
9. Is a foreign language commonly spoken in your home? ......
10. Does your mother have a job outside of your home? ......
11. Did your mother attend High School? ......
12. Did your father attend High School? ......
13. Where was your mother born? Give state or country ....
14. Where was your father born? Give state or country ....
15. List below the two things you *most commonly* do for fun during the evening. ....
16. List all the things which you do in the evening for fun and in which your mother or father take part.
    ....
    ....
    ....
17. How often have you gone to the movies (not counting movies during the school day) in the past year? Check on the dotted line *after* the most correct answer. Never been......; Been only a few times......; Go once a month......; Go twice a month......; Three times a month......; Once a week......; Twice a week.....; Three times a week......; Four times a week......; Five or more times a week.......

18. How often have you gone to movies (other than movies during the school day) this fall since school began? ....
19. Do you usually go alone to movies? ...... Do you usually go with your father or mother? ......
20. How often does your father go to movies? ......
21. How often does your mother go to movies? ....
22. Do your parents urge you to go to the movies? ......
23. Do your parents discourage your going to the movies? ....
24. Does the motion picture theater to which you go put on extra acts such as vaudeville? ...... If there is vaudeville, which do you like best, the movie or vaudeville? ....
25. If you had your own way, would you go more often to the movies? ....
26. What kind of movies do you like best? ....
27. If you go to movies two or more times a week, why do you go so often? If you go to the movies less than twice a week, why don't you go more? Answer the question which applies to your case.
....
....
....
28. How many books (other than schoolbooks) have you read during the past month? ....
29. How many dances have you gone to the past month? ....
30. How many evenings a week do you spend away from home? ......
31. How many magazines do you read regularly? ...... Name them:
....

THE ATTITUDES TESTS

INSTRUCTIONS

Do not sign your name anywhere.
Write here the letter on your admission card ....
Are you a boy or girl? ....
How old are you? ....
Name of your home-room teacher ....

We are going to ask you some questions this morning to find out what you think about certain things. And we want to know what *your* real opinion is and what *you really* think. Accordingly, we have arranged that you do not need to sign your name. There will be no way for any of your teachers to find out what you have said. So feel free to answer the questions as accurately as you possibly can.

Do not ask questions unless you do not understand the directions.

Appendix C

There will be a second set of questions to be filled out. We will announce later when this will be done.

When the second set of questions has been filled out we will tell you what this is all about.

Ballot No. II

Form A

VOTE by drawing a line under one of the words printed at the left of each statement. Any one of the words would make sense but only one will express your opinion.

SAMPLE: <u>All</u> Most Many Some Few No apples have seeds.
All apples have seeds so "all" should be underlined.

1. All Most Many Some Few No examinations tend to make pupils dishonest.
2. All Most Many Some Few No Spaniards are too romantic and impractical.
3. All Most Many Some Few No Chinese are cunning and underhand.
4. All Most Many Some Few No murderers escape their just punishment.
5. All Most Many Some Few No hold-up men are brave, dare-devil fellows, out for adventure.
6. All Most Many Some Few No dancers lead most fascinating lives.
7. All Most Many Some Few No people who go to big football games get drunk.
8. All Most Many Some Few No marriages are unsuccessful.
9. All Most Many Some Few No professional dancers are decent folk.
10. All Most Many Some Few No criminals are courageous, brave, and nervy.
11. All Most Many Some Few No football games are occasions at which many people get drunk.
12. All Most Many Some Few No Japanese should be kept out of the United States.
13. All Most Many Some Few No schoolbooks are interesting.
14. All Most Many Some Few No thieves are honorable in their dealings with others of their kind.

15. All	Most	Many	Some	Few	No	cowboys are heavy drinkers.
16. All	Most	Many	Some	Few	No	Italians readily become the tools of criminal gangs.
17. All	Most	Many	Some	Few	No	Mexicans are bandits.
18. All	Most	Many	Some	Few	No	chorus girls are worth-while members of society.
19. All	Most	Many	Some	Few	No	Italians are desirable citizens for the United States.
20. All	Most	Many	Some	Few	No	adult men of the country have not tasted a drop of liquor since the passage of the prohibition amendment.
21. No	Few	Some	Many	Most	All	law-breakers in the end turn out to be decent citizens.
22. No	Few	Some	Many	Most	All	prize fighters are unworthy of anyone's admiration.
23. No	Few	Some	Many	Most	All	adult men of this country have been drunk one or more times since the passage of the prohibition amendment.
24. No	Few	Some	Many	Most	All	school principals know their job.
25. No	Few	Some	Many	Most	All	professional athletes care little about the game.
26. No	Few	Some	Many	Most	All	school readers are full of dull stories.
27. No	Few	Some	Many	Most	All	wars have brought untold suffering to human beings.
28. No	Few	Some	Many	Most	All	marriages are successful even if the husband fails to earn a decent wage.
29. No	Few	Some	Many	Most	All	criminals are clever and would make a good living honestly if they wanted to.
30. No	Few	Some	Many	Most	All	Japanese readily become the tools of criminal gangs.
31. No	Few	Some	Many	Most	All	college men would take a drink if it were offered to them in private.
32. No	Few	Some	Many	Most	All	other pupils in this school are good-natured.

Appendix C

33. No	Few	Some	Many	Most	All	Russians are greedy and cruel.
34. No	Few	Some	Many	Most	All	prohibition agents are honest and conscientious.
35. No	Few	Some	Many	Most	All	college professors are strong, robust men.
36. No	Few	Some	Many	Most	All	school teachers are too hard with their pupils.
37. No	Few	Some	Many	Most	All	college professors are most impractical.
38. No	Few	Some	Many	Most	All	Italians are quick to repay injury with revenge.
39. No	Few	Some	Many	Most	All	laborers would have wine in their cellar if they could afford it.
40. No	Few	Some	Many	Most	All	doctors in the country are prescribing alcohol to people who really don't need it.
41. All	Most	Many	Some	Few	No	rum runners are clever fellows out for adventure.
42. All	Most	Many	Some	Few	No	Frenchmen are ladies' men.
43. All	Most	Many	Some	Few	No	prohibition agents are religious fanatics.
44. All	Most	Many	Some	Few	No	Protestant ministers are highly intelligent.
45. All	Most	Many	Some	Few	No	children would stay away from a party rather than wear shabby clothes.
46. All	Most	Many	Some	Few	No	smartly dressed girls are popular.
47. All	Most	Many	Some	Few	No	policemen are rough and bullying to people whom they get into their power.
48. All	Most	Many	Some	Few	No	school subjects are interesting.
49. All	Most	Many	Some	Few	No	husbands and wives quarrel all the time.
50. All	Most	Many	Some	Few	No	athletes are to be admired.
51. All	Most	Many	Some	Few	No	Arab chieftains are handsome men.
52. All	Most	Many	Some	Few	No	policemen torture and mistreat anyone suspected of a crime.

Appendix C

53. All	Most	Many	Some	Few	No	policemen are courteous and well intentioned.
54. All	Most	Many	Some	Few	No	Russians are desirable citizens for the United States.
55. All	Most	Many	Some	Few	No	persons who want liquor have no difficulty in getting it.
56. All	Most	Many	Some	Few	No	college professors are sickly, weak men who have to wear glasses.
57. All	Most	Many	Some	Few	No	husbands buy little presents for their wives occasionally.
58. All	Most	Many	Some	Few	No	farmers of this country make their own wine.
59. All	Most	Many	Some	Few	No	Arabs are terrible fighters.
60. All	Most	Many	Some	Few	No	Mexicans are civilized.
61. All	Most	Many	Some	Few	No	Mexicans are upright citizens and honest men.
62. All	Most	Many	Some	Few	No	robbers escape their just punishment.
63. All	Most	Many	Some	Few	No	social workers are meddlers.
64. All	Most	Many	Some	Few	No	sea captains are loyal and true.

BALLOT No. III

FORM A

This portion of the ballots contains a great variety of questions. *Read carefully to see what is asked for EACH time.* Indicate your answers by check marks.

1. The police commissioner padlocked a hundred night clubs for selling liquor. If both of the following things were to happen, which would be the most important? Check the most important thing.
......The night club owners lost a lot of money.
......The city developed a new respect for law.

2. What are some good reasons for a boy continuing to go with a girl? Check the *two* best reasons in the following list. Both boys and girls please answer.
......When her father has a lot of money.
......When she is content with inexpensive entertainment.
......When she permits him to kiss her good night.
......When she dolls up and looks nice for him.
......When she refuses to let the other fellows make love to her.

3. A certain city started on a program of strict enforcement of the prohibition laws. If both the following things were to happen which would be the most important? Check one.
   ......The city grew to respect law and authority.
   ......A thousand men were unable to get their drinks.
4. Which would you rather be? Check one.
   ......A college professor.
   ......A popular actor.
5. What would you rather do?
   ......Give money to a good cause.
   ......Loan money to a friend.
6. Ruth put all her money in the bank. If both of the following things were to happen, which would be the most important?
   ......She had money when she grew up.
   ......She had money when any help was needed for people in trouble.
7. When is a boy justified in breaking with his best girl? In the following list check the *two* best reasons for a boy refusing to go any more with his best girl. (Girls please answer also.)
   ......When her father loses his money and she has to get a job.
   ......When she wants to go to the most expensive show in town every week.
   ......When she refuses to kiss him good night.
   ......When she refuses to doll up and look smart.
   ......When she lets the other fellows kiss her.
8. What do you most dislike? In the following list check the *three* things you would most dislike having to do.
   ......Having to miss dinner.
   ......Having to watch a prize fight.
   ......Having to pass a drunken man on the street.
   ......Having to help a slow child with his lessons.
   ......Having to say good-by to your best friend.
   ......Having to read about a terrible famine in China.
9. Dick and Betty had led rather disreputable lives. Their ship took fire in mid-ocean. They realized that the end was near and promised to reform if they were saved. What is most likely to happen?
   ......The ship burned up and all on board were lost.
   ......A sudden cloudburst of rain put out the fire.
10. There was much drinking at a certain football game. If both the following things were to happen, which would be the most important?

......The good names of the two colleges were harmed.
......A score of men had to be locked up in jail and missed important business engagements.

11. John Hunter was the leading athlete and ladies' man of the senior class. At a dance in a neighboring town a girl made eyes at him, but when John asked her to dance with him, she refused. What is John *most likely* to do?
......Compel her to dance with him anyway.
......Leave her alone.

12. Below are short descriptions of some Junior High boys whom you may know. Check the *two* whom you most dislike.
......The class athlete; he knows it all too well.
......Always picking on others.
......The "petter" and "necker."
......Flares up and gets mad on the least excuse.

13. What do you most thoroughly dislike? In the following list check the *four* things you dislike most.
......Laws restricting the liberty of the individual
......Drinking parties
......Unemployment
......Losing your best friend
......A famine in India
......Ragged clothing
......Drinking by men
......Military ambitions

14. Tom Larson was a wealthy Arizona ranch owner. He had been losing cattle and suspected cattle rustling. While investigating the loss of his cattle, he found himself surrounded by bandits. The bandits locked him up in an abandoned mine and told him that in a week his cattle would be driven across the border. What is most likely to happen?
......Tom finds a secret exit from the mine, gathers a posse, and captures the bandits just as they are about to cross the border.
......Tom is unable to escape in time and loses all his cattle.

15. Joe Henderson was a well educated and cultured man who had had hard luck. He had sunk to the level of running a cheap dance hall in Chinatown and grew so powerful that he could order a man shot at will. He suddenly closed up his dance hall and went straight. What is the most probable reason for his sudden change?

APPENDIX C

...... He was afraid that eventually the police would find him out and send him to prison.
...... He fell in love with a girl who made him see what kind of life he was living.

16. If a poor girl comes to school in ragged clothes, what is the best thing to do?
    ...... Pay no attention to her.
    ...... Persuade someone who is clever with a needle to help her make some new clothes.

17. Below are short descriptions of Junior High School girls whom you may know. Check the *two* whom you most dislike.
    ...... Boy crazy.
    ...... Is proud of the fact that she dares to smoke cigarettes.
    ...... The class giggler, she laughs and giggles at everything.
    ...... The innocent one, so ignorant of the world that she is always asking foolish questions.

18. When is a girl justified in throwing over her best fellow? In the following list check the *two* best reasons for a girl refusing to go any more with a boy. (Boys please answer also.)
    ...... When he gets serious and wants to marry her.
    ...... When he proves that he can't hold a job of any kind.
    ...... When he wants to kiss her good night.
    ...... When he gets angry and scolds.
    ...... When he is too free in making love to other girls.

19. What do you most thoroughly dislike? In the following list check the *three* things you dislike most.
    ...... Drinking by men
    ...... Unemployment
    ...... Poverty
    ...... A famine in India
    ...... Laws restricting the liberty of the individual
    ...... Military ambitions
    ...... Having to miss dinner

20. What would you rather do in a baseball game?
    ...... Hit a home run.
    ...... Help make a double play.

21. Which of the following girls would you rather have for a friend? Check one.
    ...... Jane, who doesn't care a rap what the gang thinks when she refuses to join in their fun and mischief.
    ...... Dorothy, who is all for doing what her gang wants to do no matter what it is.

22. What are the traits most desirable in a mother? Check the *two* most desirable traits in the following list.
      ......Being a good cook and housekeeper
      ......Being prominent in social life
      ......Respecting her children's opinions
      ......Always having time to read, talk, or play with her children
      ......Being a college graduate
      ......Never losing her temper or nagging

23. Mike was the captain of a ship in the South Seas. A girl in a dance hall made love to him, but when Mike wanted her to go to sea with him she refused. What *should* Mike *do?*
      ......Curse his bad luck and go back to his ship without her.
      ......Smash the lamps in the dance hall and carry the girl off by force.

24. A boy is being teased by some other children. What is the best thing to do?
      ......Tell them they ought to be ashamed to pick on somebody like that.
      ......Propose something everybody can play, so they won't think about teasing.

25. Ruth had saved up $5 for skates she wanted very much. When she heard about the starving children in Russia, she gladly gave her $5 to help out. What is most likely to happen?
      ......When the other girls had skates she was sorry she did not have $5 to buy some too.
      ......She found a pair of skates for being so kind.

26. What would you rather do?
      ......Sing in a school quartet
      ......Sing a solo at school

27. Ruth had saved up $5 for skates she wanted very much. When she heard about the starving children in Russia, she gladly gave her $5 to help out. What is most likely to happen?
      ......She had no skates that winter.
      ......Her father appreciated her generous act and bought her a pair.

28. Your class has been asked to raise twenty-five dollars for a school memorial. What is the best way to raise the money?
      ......Tax every one of the fifty pupils in the room fifty cents apiece.
      ......Put on a class play and raise the money that way.

29. If some one calls you names, what is the best thing to do?
 ......Do him some favor to show him that you are not as bad as he thinks.
 ......Make him apologize or give him a good licking.
30. Jim and the boys used to ride down the steep sidewalk very fast on their wagons and scooters and then turn the corner very sharply. What is most likely to happen?
 ......It made other people uncomfortable seeing them do it.
 ......They tipped over and Jim was badly scratched up.
31. Harry got into fights on the playground and streets. If both of the following things were to happen, which would be the most important?
 ......Other boys were afraid of him.
 ......The boys all cheered him when he fought.

BALLOT No. II

FORM B

VOTE by drawing a line under one of the words printed at the left of each statement. Any one of the words would make sense but only one will express your opinion.

SAMPLE: No Few Some Many Most <u>All</u> apples have seeds.
 All apples have seeds so "all" should be underlined.

1. No Few Some Many Most All policemen are ridiculous and boastful fellows.
2. No Few Some Many Most All attractive girls wear smart clothes.
3. No Few Some Many Most All Frenchmen are romantic love-makers.
4. No Few Some Many Most All criminals, when sentenced to death, escape with last-minute pardons.
5. No Few Some Many Most All school rules should be changed.
6. No Few Some Many Most All detectives are unable to follow clues as they should.
7. No Few Some Many Most All sea captains are brave.
8. No Few Some Many Most All Frenchmen are impractical.
9. No Few Some Many Most All persons should be thrilled at the sight of marching soldiers.

Appendix C

10. No Few Some Many Most All — teachers are too easy with their pupils.
11. No Few Some Many Most All — people who break the law finally reform.
12. No Few Some Many Most All — people who vote dry practice what they vote.
13. No Few Some Many Most All — gang leaders are real men.
14. No Few Some Many Most All — marriages are unsuccessful if the man is unable to earn a decent wage.
15. No Few Some Many Most All — criminals reform and turn out in the end to be decent citizens.
16. No Few Some Many Most All — soldiers are benefited by the strict discipline of preparing for war.
17. No Few Some Many Most All — Japanese are desirable citizens for the United States.
18. No Few Some Many Most All — persons who have the money can buy a drink in any large city in the land.
19. No Few Some Many Most All — chorus girls are to be admired.
20. No Few Some Many Most All — people are benefited by learning the lesson of wartime discipline.
21. All Most Many Some Few No — people would rather steal than wear shabby clothes.
22. All Most Many Some Few No — social reformers have the the best interests of every one at heart.
23. All Most Many Some Few No — social workers are busybodies.
24. All Most Many Some Few No — chorus girls lead shady lives.
25. All Most Many Some Few No — Mexicans are dirty, evil-looking fellows.
26. All Most Many Some Few No — Chinese are frank and fair and square.
27. All Most Many Some Few No — gang leaders are fine-looking fellows with good manners and generous ways.

Appendix C

28. All Most Many Some Few No robbers are chivalrous and tender hearted toward women and children.
29. All Most Many Some Few No Russians are kind and generous.
30. All Most Many Some Few No small town police officials are clever and efficient.
31. All Most Many Some Few No Chinese who live in America are easily excited to fighting among themselves.
32. All Most Many Some Few No criminals escape their just punishment.
33. All Most Many Some Few No criminals are cowards in the face of danger.
34. All Most Many Some Few No men who work hard will accumulate comfortable wealth.
35. All Most Many Some Few No textbooks are interesting.
36. All Most Many Some Few No school subjects are well taught.
37. All Most Many Some Few No senators who are politically dry have wine in their own cellars.
38. All Most Many Some Few No large cities in the west are so dry that a drink cannot be bought at any price.
39. All Most Many Some Few No pupils like to go to school.
40. All Most Many Some Few No Japanese are rich men's servants.
41. All Most Many Some Few No parties these days have something besides punch to drink.
42. All Most Many Some Few No Arab chieftains are fierce fighters.
43. All Most Many Some Few No criminals have good qualities mixed with the bad.
44. All Most Many Some Few No Spaniards are love-makers.
45. No Few Some Many Most All Spaniards are desirable citizens for the United States.
46. No Few Some Many Most All crooks play fair with others of their own kind.
47. No Few Some Many Most All criminals have better than average intelligence.

APPENDIX C

48. No Few Some Many Most All crooks could make a living honestly if they wanted to.
49. No Few Some Many Most All Chinese readily become the tools of criminal gangs.
50. No Few Some Many Most All prohibition agents are "wild-eyed" reformers.
51. No Few Some Many Most All beautiful women who commit crimes escape punishment.
52. No Few Some Many Most All cowboys are dirty, mean, and lazy.
53. No Few Some Many Most All differences between nations can be settled by peaceful methods.
54. No Few Some Many Most All girls would stay at home rather than go to a dance in an ordinary dress.
55. No Few Some Many Most All prize fighters are to be admired.
56. No Few Some Many Most All Arabs are cruel and greedy.
57. No Few Some Many Most All college professors could do well in business if they wanted to.
58. No Few Some Many Most All dances are occasions at which several people get drunk.
59. No Few Some Many Most All Mexicans are half-breeds.
60. No Few Some Many Most All supporters of prohibition are too ready to ignore the rights of the other fellow.
61. No Few Some Many Most All supporters of prohibition have the welfare of the whole country at heart.
62. No Few Some Many Most All cowboys are loyal and true friends.
63. No Few Some Many Most All Protestant ministers are below average intelligence.
64. No Few Some Many Most All small-town detectives couldn't follow a clue if it were shown to them.
65. No Few Some Many Most All modern parties are complete without wine to drink.

Appendix C

Ballot No. III

Form B

This portion of the ballots contains a great variety of questions. *Read carefully to see what is asked for each time.* Indicate your answers by check marks.

1. Ruth put all her money in the bank. If both of the following things were to happen, which would be the most important?
    - ...... She did not need to ask her father and mother for money whenever she needed it.
    - ...... Every day her father gave her a nickel to add to her account.

2. Henry worked hard and saved his money until by the time he was twenty-five years old he was very well fixed financially. What is most likely to happen?
    - ...... He became more and more generous with his money the more he had.
    - ...... He became more and more selfish with his money.

3. An American heiress was lost in the Sahara and picked up by a band of Arab bandits. What is most likely to happen?
    - ...... She is held prisoner until a large ransom is paid.
    - ...... The French Foreign Legion surprises the band, puts its leaders in irons, and frees the American heiress.

4. What are the traits most desirable in a father? Check the *two* most desirable traits in the following list.
    - ...... Being a college graduate
    - ...... Spending time with his children, reading, talking, playing with them
    - ...... Making plenty of money
    - ...... Owning a good-looking car
    - ...... Never nagging his children about what they do
    - ...... Respecting his children's opinions

5. An American explorer unintentionally violated the code of a certain African tribe and was sentenced to be thrown to a huge alligator which was worshiped by the tribe. What is most likely to happen?
    - ...... The explorer is given to the alligator who devours him.
    - ...... The American works a trick of quickly grabbing the nose of the alligator so the beast cannot breathe and thus saves his life.

6. What are the sources of disagreement between you and your parents? Check *all* the items in the following list which cause disagreements between you and your parents.
    ......Use of the family automobile
    ......The boys or girls you choose as your friends
    ......Your spending money
    ......Number of times you go out on school nights
    ......Your school grades
    ......The hour you get in at night
    ......Home duties (tending furnace, washing dishes)
    ......The way you dress
    ......Smoking
    ......Your "dates"

7. Here is a list of things which boys and girls sometimes do. Check what seem to you the *three worst* ones in the following list.
    ......Smoking cigarettes
    ......Cheating on examinations
    ......Telling smutty stories
    ......Swearing
    ......Stealing
    ......Petting and necking
    ......Destroying school property
    ......Bullying
    ......Fist fighting
    ......Pushing and shoving while in line

8. How soon should a girl begin to think of getting married? Check one answer.
    ......Before she is twenty years old
    ......Between twenty and twenty-five
    ......After twenty-five

9. The fourth-grade pupils could not agree where to go for their spring class picnic. What is the best way to decide?
    ......Put the problem up to the teacher and let her decide.
    ......Appoint two pupils to go to both picnicking places and instruct them to report which is the best.

10. There is much drinking among the students at a certain college. If both the following things were to happen, which would be the *most* important?
    ......The students didn't learn much.
    ......The people of the country lost some trained leaders.

APPENDIX C   123

11. John started across the street without looking both ways. What is most likely to happen?
......He caused an accident to other people.
......He got across as safely as anyone.

12. What do you thoroughly dislike? In the following list check the *three* things you dislike most.
......Ragged clothing
......Cruelty to animals
......Losing your best friend
......Drinking by women
......Ignorance
......Drinking parties
......Gambling on horse races

13. Below are short descriptions of some Junior High School girls whom you may know. Check the *two* whom you most dislike.
......The class snob—looks down on the rest of the pupils.
......This girl can be kissed by any boy who has a little nerve.
......The class beauty, she knows it all too well.
......" Fatty," she eats too much candy and is shabbily dressed.

14. There was a great famine in India causing hundreds of people to die. What is the best thing to do?
......Give what money you have saved to a relief organization such as the Red Cross.
......Join in some benefit performance or class work to raise money.

15. Below are some short descriptions of Junior High School boys whom you may know. Check the *two* that you most dislike.
......Always has a smutty or dirty story to tell
......Teacher's pet
......Always borrowing and never returning
......Practical joker, his favorite is to put a tack in your seat.

16. Ruth had saved up $5 for skates she wanted very much. When she heard about the starving children in Russia she gladly gave her $5 to help out. If both of the following things were to happen, which would be the most important?
......She found another pair for being so kind.
......It made the Russian children happy when the money came.

17. John Hunter was the leading athlete and ladies' man o' the senior class. At a dance in a neighboring town a girl made eyes at him, but

when John asked her to dance with him she refused. What *should* John *do?*

...... Leave her alone
...... Insist that she dance with him

18. A prize of $100 was offered for the best esssy on the League of Nations. The sponsors of the plan provided a great many books and articles for the children to read. When the teacher explained the prize offer to her class two plans for winning the prize were proposed. Check which one you think is the better.

...... Each pupil was to work by himself and submit his own essay and try to win the prize for himself.

...... The three best writers of the group were to prepare the essay while the rest of the class was to read and make notes on the books and articles. If the essay prepared by the class won, the money was to be divided equally among all.

19. If some one pushes and shoves on the street car, what is the best thing to do?

...... Give him a push back
...... Pay no attention to him

20. Which of the following people would you like to know more about?

...... Helen Hunter, who is beginning her medical training.
...... Sally O'Dare, who is just getting her first chance in a Broadway show.

21. Which would you rather be?

...... A college professor
...... A cowboy

22. Mike was the captain of a ship in the South Seas. He fell in love with a girl in a dance hall. He wanted her to go to sea with him but she refused. What is *most likely* to happen?

...... Mike cursed his bad luck and went back to his ship without her.
...... Mike and his crew smashed the lamps in the dance hall and in the confusion carried the girl off by force.

23. Which of the following things should you get permission from your parents to do? Check on the dotted line all the things you should get permission to do before you do them.

1. ...... To smoke

2. ...... To stay out after nine o'clock

3. ...... To go to school on a rainy day without your rubbers

Appendix C

4. ......To go to a school picnic
5. ......To go with the school football team to another town
6. ......To stay out for a meal
7. ......To visit a friend
8. ......To use the family automobile
9. ......To buy some clothes
10. ......To visit a stranger
11. ......To go into debt for something
12. ......To visit a neighbor
13. ......To read a novel
14. ......To go to the movies
15. ......To buy ice cream or candy
16. ......To go to a dance
17. ......To make a "date"
18. ......To give your own money to the Red Cross
19. ......To visit the pantry and eat between meals
20. ......To charge things to your parents' account at a store
21. ......To go to another town with a friend for the day
22. ......To go to visit a distant friend
23 ......To spend ten cents for candy
24. ......To take the basketball team to another town with the family car
25. ......To go to a school dance
26. ......To go to a dance in a neighboring town
27. ......To pledge ten dollars to the Red Cross
28. ......To buy a suit or dress and charge it
29. ......To borrow lunch money from a friend
30. ......To buy a fountain pen
31. ......To stay out after ten o'clock
32. ......To stay after school half an hour
33. ......To get a steady job working Saturdays

24. How soon should a man begin to think of getting married? Check one answer.
    ...... Before he is twenty years old
    ...... Between twenty and twenty-five
    ...... After twenty-five
25. "Scar-faced" Johnson had led a criminal career all his life. He suddenly quit the game and went straight. What is the most probable explanation of his sudden change?
    ...... He was afraid the police would eventually get him.
    ...... He fell in love with a girl who insisted that he go straight.
26. What are some good reasons for a girl continuing to go with a boy? Check the *two* best reasons in the following list.
    ...... When he gets serious and wants to marry her
    ...... When he proves that he can hold a job
    ...... When he wants to kiss her good night
    ...... When he is always a good sport
    ...... When he leaves the other girls alone

BALLOT No. I

WHAT DO YOU THINK IS TRUE

Read each statement carefully and underline the word "True" if it seems to you to be true. Underline the word "False" if it seems to you to be false.

SAMPLE: It is a good thing to do a good turn every day. <u>True</u> False
    The above statement is true, and the word "True" is underlined.

1. The nation with a large military force will be tempted to use it..True False
2. Few people get drunk these days at football games.......True False
3. A man who is respected in his community can do a lot of harm by taking an occasional drink..................True False
4. It should be left to counties, townships, and cities whether they wish to permit the sale of alcohol, beer, and wine....True False
5. The prominent citizen who violates the law can do a lot of harm by destroying people's faith in him...............True False
6. Gang leaders are usually fine-looking fellows with good manners and generous ways........................True False

APPENDIX C

7. It is no one's business if a reputable citizen takes an occasional drink..................................True False
8. It is your duty to stick with your gang even when they go wrong..................................True False
9. Only a very few Japanese are desirable citizens of the United States..................................True False
10. If a man wants to take an occasional drink it is his own business..................................True False
11. Many criminals reform and turn out in the end to be decent citizens..................................True False
12. The best-dressed boy or girl in the class is usually the most popular..................................True False
13. Few adult men have tasted liquor since the passage of the prohibition amendment..................................True False
14. A little rouge, high heels, and smart clothes add to the attractiveness of a girl..................................True False
15. Most Russians are kind and generous..................True False
16. Most criminals are courageous, brave, and nervy........True False
17. Most prize fighters are unworthy of anyone's admiration..True False
18. Marching should thrill every heart....................True False
19. Few Chinese are frank and fair and square.............True False
20. A thief is always a coward...........................True False
21. Most supporters of prohibition have the welfare of the whole country at heart..................................True False
22. A man has to have real intelligence to plan a robbery.....True False
23. Even murderers frequently reform and become worthwhile citizens..................................True False
24. Anyone who has the money can buy a drink in any large city in the land..................................True False
25. Hard work is not enough to win a fortune..............True False
26. Most policemen are rough and bullying to people whom they get into their power..................................True False
27. Successful marriage is chiefly dependent upon a large enough financial income..................................True False

28. Those who work hard will amass a fortune..............True False
29. Most Italians are desirable citizens for the United States..True False
30. Good clothes help to make the man.................True False
31. We cannot hope to do away with war, because it is a part of the unending struggle for survival in a crowded world..True False
32. Few criminals are clever enough to make a good living honestly even if they wanted to......................True False
33. Marriage usually ends in failure if the husband is unable to earn a decent wage.............................True False
34. War is the most terrible thing that can happen to our present civilization..............................True False
35. The most popular girl in class is usually the best dressed..True False
36. A modern party is not complete unless there is something besides punch to drink...........................True False
37. The girl without a party dress is out of place at a dance...True False
38. Most Arab chieftains are handsome men, hard riders, and fierce fighters...................................True False
39. Few small-town police are clever and efficient...........True False
40. It is no one's business if a man carries a hip flask of liquor.True False
41. The most popular boy in class is rarely the best dressed.True False
42. The soldier suffers tremendously and gains very little...True False
43. Enforcement of prohibition should be left to the separate states..True False

APPENDIX D

TABLES SHOWING DIFFERENCES IN THE ATTITUDES OF MOVIE AND NON-MOVIE CHILDREN

THE accompanying tables present detailed summaries of the results of testing attitudes of movie and non-movie children. Fifteen comparisons of movie and non-movie children were made for all items. Movie boys were compared with non-movie boys, movie girls with non-movie girls, and movie boys and girls with non-movie boys and girls for each of the four populations and for the populations combined. The accompanying tables present the data for only the combined populations supplemented by notes indicating any peculiarities of the separate populations. Where all four populations were tested about 400 non-movie cases are compared with 400 movie cases. Four populations, however, are not available for all items, since among the 341 items the Troup children responded to only 147 and since superintendents were asked to strike out items which they thought unsuitable for their groups. All together over 400,000 responses to test elements have been tabulated in reaching these results. Some general comments are in order before presenting the detail of the data.

The results of the attitude survey show probably significant differences on 45 test items. These are items showing differences four or more times as large as their probable errors or any one of the final comparisons. Only 20 items show differences five or more times as large as their probable errors and only 5 items show differences seven or more times as large as their probable errors. Due to limitations of space detailed data on only 20 questions are presented. Although there are 45 items showing probably significant differences in the statistical sense of not being explainable on the ground of sampling errors, *the actual differences in terms of percentages are in general small.* The most significant difference is only 22.4 per cent and several items showing a difference of only

9 per cent are classified as probably significant. That test items showing such small differences are statistically significant is due to the large number of cases tested. That is, a distinction must be drawn between differences which are meaningful and significant in the usual sense and differences which are significant in a statistical sense. Given a sufficient number of cases even a very small difference would be statistically significant, but such a small difference might carry no general significance whatever for guiding efforts to improve the child's environment.

Probable errors have been calculated from the formula

$$.6745\sqrt{\sigma_2^1 + \sigma_2^2}.$$

In the case of distributions of the All-Most-Many-Some-Few-No-type the procedure has been to group the responses into a four-fold table at the point which would give the most significant difference. This tends slightly to overstate the differences. On the other hand it should be observed that community differences tend to obscure differences between movie and non-movie attenders. An extreme case will illustrate this tendency. To the statement "Football games are occasions at which many people get drunk" we have the following percentage distribution of replies from movie and non-movie children in three populations. (This item was not given to Dayton children.)

	All	Most	Many	Some	Few	No
Troup						
NM	8	12	16	29	17	18
M	12	18	24	15	9	22
Norwalk						
NM	2	3	5	19	22	49
M	1	2	5	19	31	42
Fair Haven						
NM	1	5	13	29	25	27
M	4	5	24	34	21	12

In all three populations the movie children tend to respond on the positive end of the scale, "All" or "Most" or "Many," while the non-movie cases tend to respond on the opposite or negative end of the scale. It is apparent that there are large differences between the populations and that these differences shift the point at which movie and non-movie cases differ. The influence of shifting the point of division may be shown by regrouping the above data as follows:

Troup	All, Most, Many	Some, Few, No
NM	36	64
M	54	46
Norwalk	All, Most, Many, Some, Few	No
NM	51	49
M	58	42
Fair Haven	All, Most, Many, Some	Some, Few
NM	48	52
M	67	33

Using this division and combining we have the following:

	Tendency to Positive Response	Tendency to Negative Response
NM	45	55
M	60	40

This yields a difference of 15 per cent. But combination without grouping yields the following distributions, showing only a 9 per cent difference when the point of division is between "some" and "few."

	All	Most	Many	Some	Few	No
NM	3.3	6.9	11.3	26.0	21.6	30.9
M	5.5	8.1	17.0	22.4	20.5	26.6

We have experimented with regrouping the responses to similar items. In every case the percentage difference which results is larger. However, after this procedure has been applied to four or five of the most obvious cases, we immediately encounter the difficulty that this procedure may be creating differences where none exist instead of clarifying differences.

The following tables present the percentage distribution of the responses of non-movie boys (NMB), movie boys (MB), non-movie girls (NMG), movie girls (MG), non-movie boys and girls

(NM) and movie boys and girls (M). The italicized percentages are significantly larger and indicate the characteristic and differential attitudes of the contrasted groups.

TABLE 1

Which would you rather be? Check one.

(a) A college professor
(b) A popular actor

	a	b	Total %	N	C.R.
NMB	*72.0*	28.0	100	221	
MB	52.7	*47.3*	100	205	6.0
NMG	*66.4*	33.6	100	208	
MG	41.8	*58.2*	100	203	7.2
NM	*69.2*	30.8	100	429	
M	47.3	*52.7*	100	408	9.5

Troup, Norwalk, Fair Haven, Dayton consistent throughout.
This is one of the two most significant differences found.
C.R. is the Critical Ratio, the difference being 9.5 times its probable error

TABLE 2

Which of the following people would you like to know more about?

(a) Helen Hunter, who is beginning her medical training
(b) Sally O'Dare, who is just getting her first chance in a Broadway show

	a	b	Total %	N	C.R.
NMB	*69.0*	31.0	100	206	
MB	53.5	*46.5*	100	198	4.7
NMG	*76.0*	24.0	100	206	
MG	47.2	*52.8*	100	193	8.7
NM	*72.7*	27.3	100	412	
M	50.3	*49.7*	100	391	9.7

Troup, Norwalk, Fair Haven, Dayton.
This is the most significant difference found. With the exception of Norwalk boys, it is consistent throughout.

Appendix D

Table 3
College professors are strong, robust men.

	All	Most	Many	Some	Few	No	Total %	N	C.R.
NMB	2.4	16.2	19.8	36.5	21.6	3.6	100.1	167	
MB	4.6	10.5	11.1	37.3	32.7	3.9	100.1	153	4.1
NMG	6.3	15.1	21.4	42.1	12.6	2.5	100	159	
MG	4.8	13.6	10.9	48.3	16.3	6.1	100	147	3.6
NM	4.3	15.7	20.6	39.3	17.2	3.1	100.2	326	
M	4.7	12.0	11.0	42.7	24.7	5.0	100.1	300	5.5

Norwalk, Fair Haven, Dayton.
The tendency is consistent through all three populations.

Table 4
Chorus girls are worth-while members of society.

	All	Most	Many	Some	Few	No	Total %	N	C.R.
NMB	8.1	9.9	21.1	28.7	22.8	9.4	100	223	
MB	4.9	7.4	13.3	28.6	34.0	11.8	100	203	4.2
NMG	5.9	13.7	18.1	29.3	26.4	6.8	100.2	205	
MG	6.1	8.2	8.2	29.1	34.7	13.8	100.1	196	4.6
NM	7.0	11.7	19.7	29.0	24.6	8.2	100.2	430	
M	5.5	7.8	10.8	28.9	34.4	12.8	100.2	399	6.4

Troup, Norwalk, Fair Haven, Dayton.
This is one of the eleven most significant items. The tendency is consistent for boys and girls and for all four populations. The result is precisely opposite to our original hypothesis that movies tended to glorify the chorus girl.

Table 5
Cowboys are dirty, mean, and lazy.

	All	Most	Many	Some	Few	No	Total %	N	C.R.
NMB	2.9	2.4	5.9	23.3	47.6	18.8	99.9	170	
MB	2.0	2.7	3.4	18.1	61.8	12.1	100.1	149	4.0
NMG	1.9	3.8	3.2	39.5	33.8	17.8	100	157	
MG	.7	5.0	5.7	28.4	48.0	12.1	99.9	141	3.8
NM	2.4	3.1	4.6	30.6	41.0	18.4	100.1	327	
M	1.4	3.8	4.5	23.1	55.2	12.1	100.1	290	5.5

Norwalk, Fair Haven, Dayton.
This illustrates a difference which is difficult of interpretation because the movie children tend strongly to respond "Few" when the non-movie children pile up their responses on "Some" and "No." The Critical Ratio is based upon differences in underlining "Few."

Appendix D

Table 6

Supporters of prohibition have the welfare of the whole country at heart.

	All	Most	Many	Some	Few	No	Total %	N	C.R.
NMB	8.6	18.7	23.2	27.8	12.7	9.1	100.1	220	
MB	5.1	13.8	20.9	35.2	17.3	7.7	100	196	3.6
NMG	7.1	15.2	21.7	30.3	15.2	10.6	100.1	198	
MG	5.4	10.2	17.2	37.1	22.6	7.5	100	186	4.4
NM	7.9	17.0	22.5	29.0	13.9	9.8	99.1	418	
M	5.2	12.1	19.1	36.2	19.9	7.6	100.1	382	6.3

Troup, Norwalk, Fair Haven, Dayton.
Fair Haven is contradictory to the general tendency.

Table 7

Adult men of this country have been drunk one or more times since the passage of the prohibition amendment.

	All	Most	Many	Some	Few	No	Total %	N	C.R.
NMB	1.7	17.6	37.0	24.4	16.8	2.5	100	119	
MB	9.0	25.2	35.1	17.1	12.6	.9	99.9	111	3.7
NMG	2.6	23.3	30.2	29.3	13.8	.9	100.1	116	
MG	14.4	24.3	36.9	17.1	6.3	.9	99.9	111	4.5
NM	2.1	20.4	33.6	26.8	15.3	1.7	99.9	235	
M	11.7	24.8	36.0	17.1	9.5	.9	100	222	5.3

Norwalk, Fair Haven.
The tendency is slightly contradicted by Fair Haven girls.

Table 8

Modern parties are complete without wine to drink.

	All	Most	Many	Some	Few	No	Total %	N	C.R.
NMB	13.1	14.9	15.4	17.7	26.7	12.2	100	221	
MB	9.5	10.	14.5	16.5	33.0	16.5	100	200	3.2
NMG	19.1	13.6	14.1	14.1	30.1	9.0	100	199	
MG	14.8	6.9	11.6	14.8	31.2	20.6	99.9	189	4.6
NM	16.0	14.3	14.8	16.0	28.2	10.8	100.1	419	
M	12.1	8.5	13.1	15.7	32.1	18.5	100	389	5.0

Troup, Norwalk, Fair Haven, Dayton.
Consistent throughout.

Appendix D

Table 9

A little rouge, high heels, and smart clothes add to the attractiveness of a girl.

	True	False	Total %	N	C.R.
NMB	50.0	50.0	100	212	
MB	63.5	36.6	100.1	194	4.1
NMG	39.5	60.5	100	195	
MG	57.8	42.2	100	192	5.5
NM	45.0	55.1	100.1	407	
M	60.6	39.4	100	386	6.8

Troup, Norwalk, Fair Haven, Dayton.
The tendency is consistent throughout.

Table 10

Good clothes help to make the man.

	True	False	Total %	N	C.R.
NMB	57.5	42.6	100.1	105	
MB	65.3	34.8	100.1	187	
NMG	50.0	50.0	100.0	184	
MG	74.5	26.5	101	185	6.8
NM	53.8	46.2	100	379	
M	68.4	31.6	100	372	6.4

Troup, Norwalk, Fair Haven, Dayton.
The tendency is consistent only for girls. Only Norwalk boys show the same trend.

Table 11

Smartly dressed girls are popular.

	All	Most	Many	Some	Few	No	Total %	N	C.R.
NMB	3.6	15.5	26.8	26.8	20.2	7.1	100	168	
MB	12.0	18.9	27.7	24.5	11.3	5.7	100.1	159	5.3
NMG	7.4	13.0	17.9	34.6	18.5	8.6	100	162	
MG	10.7	23.3	20.7	23.3	14.7	7.3	100	150	4.3
NM	5.5	14.2	22.4	30.6	19.4	7.9	100	330	
M	11.3	21.1	24.3	24.0	13.0	6.5	100.2	309	5.6

Norwalk, Fair Haven, Dayton.

Appendix D

Table 12

Children would stay away from a party rather than wear shabby clothes.

	All	Most	Many	Some	Few	No	Total %	N	C.R.
NMB	12.9	25.7	*28.1*	*18.7*	10.5	4.1	100	171	
MB	9.0	*38.7*	23.2	12.9	11.0	5.2	100	155	3.7
NMG	11.2	23.0	*21.7*	*25.5*	11.8	6.8	100	161	
MG	*21.5*	*30.9*	20.8	15.4	7.4	4.0	100	149	4.8
NM	12.0	24.4	*25.0*	*22.0*	11.1	*5.4*	99.9	332	
M	*15.1*	*34.9*	22.0	14.1	9.2	4.6	99.9	304	5.2

Norwalk, Fair Haven, Dayton.
The tendency is consistent throughout.

Table 13

Mike was the captain of a ship in the South Seas. He fell in love with a girl in a dance hall. He wanted her to go to sea with him but she refused. What is most likely to happen?

(a) Mike cursed his bad luck and went back to his ship without her.
(b) Mike and his crew smashed the lamps in the dance hall and in the confusion carried the girl off by force.

	a	b	Total %	N	C.R.
NMB	*57.2*	42.8	100	215	
MB	39.0	*61.0*	100	197	5.5
NMG	77.6	22.4	100	205	
MG	62.3	*37.7*	100	194	4.6
NM	67.2	32.8	100	420	
M	50.6	*49.4*	100	391	7.2

Troup, Norwalk, Fair Haven, Dayton.
Consistent throughout.

Appendix D

Table 14

Joe Henderson was a well educated and cultured man who had had hard luck. He had sunk to the level of running a cheap dance hall in Chinatown and grew so powerful that he could order a man shot at will. He suddenly closed up his dance hall and went straight. What is the most probable reason for his sudden change?

(a) He was afraid that eventually the police would find him out and send him to prison.

(b) He fell in love with a girl who made him see what kind of a life he was living.

	a	b	Total %	N	C.R.
NMB	*36.2*	63.8	100	224	
MB	24.8	*75.2*	100	201	4.1
NMG	38.8	61.2	100	211	
MG	24.0	*76.0*	100	200	4.8
NM	*37.5*	62.5	100	435	
M	24.5	*75.5*	100	401	6.2

Troup, Norwalk, Fair Haven, Dayton.
Consistent throughout.

Table 15

"Scar-faced" Johnson had led a criminal career all his life. He suddenly quit the game and went straight. What is the most probable explanation of his sudden change?

(a) He was afraid the police would eventually get him.

(b) He fell in love with a girl who insisted that he go straight.

	a	b	Total %	N	C.R.
NMB	*43.0*	57.0	100	158	
MB	24.8	*75.2*	100	137	5.0
NMG	*38.5*	61.5	100	148	
MG	24.6	*75.4*	100	142	4.0
NM	*40.8*	59.2	100	306	
M	24.7	*75.3*	100	279	6.2

Norwalk, Fair Haven, Dayton.
The tendency is consistent throughout.

Table 16

Tom Larson was a wealthy Arizona ranch owner. He had been losing cattle and suspected cattle rustling. While investigating the loss of his cattle, he found himself surrounded by bandits. The bandits locked him up in an abandoned mine and told him that in a week his cattle would be driven across the border. What is most likely to happen?

(a) Tom finds a secret exit from the mine, gathers a posse, and captures the bandits just as they are about to cross the border.
(b) Tom is unable to escape in time and loses all his cattle.

	a	b	Total %	N	C.R.
NMB	46.8	53.2	100	224	
MB	59.6	40.4	100	203	3.9
NMG	39.6	60.4	100	204	
MG	53.5	46.7	100	199	4.1
NM	43.4	56.6	100	428	
M	56.5	43.5	100	402	5.7

Troup, Norwalk, Fair Haven, Dayton.
Fair Haven is contradictory.

Table 17

What are the sources of disagreement between you and your parents? Check all the items in the following list which cause disagreements between you and your parents.

(a) Use of the family automobile.
(b) The boys and girls you choose as your friends.

(a) Use of the family automobile.

	Checked	Omitted	Total %	N	C.R.
NMB	9.7	90.3	100	165	
MB	28.0	72.0	100	143	6.1
NMG	9.3	90.7	100	151	
MG	12.9	87.1	100	139	
NM	9.5	90.5	100	316	
M	20.6	79.4	100	282	7.5

Appendix D

(b) The boys and girls you choose as your friends.

	Checked	Omitted	Total %	N	C.R.
NMB	33.9	66.1	100	165	
MB	32.2	67.8	100	143	
NMG	21.9	78.1	100	151	
MG	41.7	58.3	100	139	5.5
NM	28.1	71.9	100	316	
M	36.9	63.1	100	282	

Norwalk, Fair Haven, Dayton.

A list of ten sources of disagreement was given. The movie children checked six of these more frequently than non-movie children and four showed no difference. The two tendencies given in detail are consistent through all three populations, although the trend does not appear with equal force for both sexes.

Table 18

Jim and the boys used to ride down the steep sidewalk very fast on their wagons and scooters and then turn the corner very sharply. What is most likely to happen?

(a) It made other people uncomfortable seeing them do it.
(b) They tipped over and Jim was badly scratched up.

	a	b	Total %	N	C.R.
NMB	33.3	66.7	100	216	
MB	18.6	81.4	100	204	5.0
NMG	36.1	63.9	100	180	
MG	17.0	83.0	100	199	6.4
NM	34.5	65.5	100	396	
M	17.8	82.2	100	403	8.3

Troup, Norwalk, Fair Haven, Dayton.

One of the three most significant items. The same tendency appeared in the data of the Character Education Inquiry, although the form of the question there was not the same.

Table 19
Schoolbooks are interesting.

	All	Most	Many	Some	Few	No	Total %	N	C.R.
NMB	20.1	*29.4*	23.2	18.3	7.1	1.8	99.9	224	
MB	20.0	19.0	24.9	18.1	*15.6*	2.4	100	205	3.7
NMG	*25.7*	*34.7*	15.7	15.2	7.1	1.4	99.8	210	
MG	24.9	23.4	*17.4*	*23.9*	8.0	*2.5*	100.1	201	3.7
NM	*22.8*	*32.1*	19.6	16.8	7.1	1.6	100	434	
M	22.4	21.2	*21.2*	*20.9*	11.8	*2.5*	100	406	5.0

Troup, Norwalk, Fair Haven, Dayton.
Norwalk slightly contradicts this tendency.

Table 20
It is your duty to stick with your gang even when they go wrong.

	True	False	Total %	N	C.R.
NMB	25.5	*74.5*	100	208	
MB	*41.7*	58.3	100	192	5.2
NMG	25.6	74.3	99.9	199	
MG	29.8	70.1	99.9	191	
NM	25.5	*74.5*	100	407	
M	*35.8*	64.2	100	383	5.0

Troup, Norwalk, Fair Haven, Dayton.
The tendency is consistent only for boys.

INDEX

Admiration or expectation not associated with approval, 44–45, 56–57
Age and differences between movie and non-movie, 79
Attitudes of movie and non-movie children toward: actors, 40–45, 137; athletes, 46; Chinese, 47–48; choice of friends, 61, 139; chorus girls, 44–45, 132, 133; cigarette smoking, 54; class giggler, 54; clothes and clothing, 6, 58, 135; college professors, 40–44, 132, 133; cowboys, 42, 45, 133; crime and criminals, 6, 51–52; criminals escaping punishment, 52; criminals reforming, 52, 55–56, 137; dancers, 44; desirable age for marriage, 53; desirable traits in father and mother, 61–62; drinking, 49–50, 64; escape from danger, 6, 62–63, 138; famine in India and China, 63–64; Frenchmen, 47–48; gang leaders, 51–52; helping a slow child, 63; heroes and "boobs" of the movies, 5, 39–47; Japanese, 47; laws restricting individual liberty, 63; losing a friend, 63; love of a woman and the reform of the criminal, 55–56, 137; marriage, 53; medical students, 44, 132; Mexicans, 47; militarism, 6, 59; movies and movie going, 67–68; offenses, 53–54; parental permission to do various things, 59–60; parents, 6, 59–62; peoples of other lands, 5, 47–49; policemen, 45; prize fighters, 46; probability, 55–56, 62–63, 136; prohibition, 5, 49–51, 134; Protestant ministers, 46–47; reasons for continuing to date with opposite sex, 54–55; rum runners, 51–52; Russians, 47–49; school, 6, 57–58, 140; sea captains, 46; sex, 6, 52–57; social workers, 46–47; sources of disagreement with parents, 61; Spaniards, 47–49; sticking with your gang, 64, 140; teachers, 57–58; thieves, 51–52; use of the family automobile, 61, 138
Attitudes tests, adequacy of, 38; administration of, 31–32; copies of, 108–128; reliability of, 34–37; selection of test items, 24–25, 27–28, 32–34; sensitivity of, 37–38

Best friends, 16–17, 26
Books, number read, 66

Character Education Inquiry, 4, 7–26, 27, 79–81
Character traits, 5, 11–12, 26
Community influence, 40, 81–82, 83, 130–131
Conduct, ratings on, 5, 11 12, 26; tests on, 5, 18–22, 26
Coöperation, 5, 17, 18–20, 26, 79–81
Correlations, frequency of movie attendance and reputation, deportment, coöperation, 81

Dances, number attended, 66
Deportment, 5, 11–13, 26, 79–81
Differences between movie and non-movie, 12–23, 39–68; summaries of, 25–26, 68–72, 82–83, 84–85

Emotional stability, 5, 25
Equating, 5, 9–11, 29–30

Frequency of movie attendance, 1, 4, 8, 11, 30–31, 77

Guess-who test, 5, 14–17, 26, 79

Hartshorne, 7
Honesty, 5, 17, 21–22, 26, 79
Hypotheses, 33, 40, 99–105

Interpretation, 85–93

141

Magazines read, 66
May, 7
Moral knowledge, 5, 22–23
Motion pictures, types of preferred by movie and non-movie, 68
Movie and non-movie children, *see* Age and; Attitudes of; Conduct; Differences between; Equating; Frequency of movie attendance of; Recreations; Reputation
Movie habits, attitudes toward, 67–68; method of collecting data on, 3, 7–8, 95–97; reasons for, 67–68; validity of reports of, 95–97. *See also* Frequency of movie attendance

Parental attitudes toward the movies, 73–75
Parental habits of movie attendance, 76–78
Parental participation in children's recreation, 76
Persistence, 5, 17, 21
Plan of the study, 1–6, 84
Populations studied, 2, 3, 7, 28–29
Pupil ratings, 5, 14–17, 26

Reading, 66
Recreations, 65–66, 107–108
Renshaw, 91
Reputation, 5, 11–18, 26, 79–81

Scholastic grade, 5, 11–12, 26, 79
Selection of movie and non-movie cases, 2–4, 8–11, 95–97, 107–108. *See also* Equating
Self-control, 5, 17, 20–21, 26
Social attitudes and opinions, 5, 23–24
Socio-economic status, 4, 5, 29, 107
Suggestibility, 25
Summaries of data, 25–26, 68–72, 82–83, 84–85

Teacher ratings, 5, 11–13, 17–18, 26
Tests, *see* Attitudes; Conduct; Reputation
Theories explaining differences between movie and non-movie, 85–93
Thurstone, 1

Validity, of attitudes tests, 34–38; of children's reports of their attendance, 95–97; of children's reports of their parents' movie attendance, 76–77